Religion at Oxford University, and Director of the Ian Ramsey Centre for Science and Religion. He holds three Oxford doctorates in the natural sciences, intellectual history and Christian theology. McGrath has written extensively on the interaction of science and Christian theology, and is the author of many books, including the international bestseller *The Dawkins Delusion? Atheist Fundamentalism and the Denial of the Divine* (SPCK, 2007), and the market-leading textbook *Christian Theology: An Introduction* (Wiley, 2016). McGrath also serves as the Gresham Professor of Divinity, a public professorship in the City of London, established in 1597, that promotes the public engagement of theology with the leading issues of the day.

ALISTER McGRATH

RICHARD DAWKINS, C. S. LEWIS
and the
MEANING
 of LIFE

spck

First published in Great Britain in 2019

Society for Promoting Christian Knowledge
36 Causton Street
London SW1P 4ST
www.spck.org.uk

British Library Cataloguing-in-Publication Data
A catalogue record for this book is available from the British Library

ISBN 978–0–281–08019–9
eBook ISBN 978–0–281–08020–5

1 3 5 7 9 10 8 6 4 2

Typeset by Manila Typesetting Company
Printed and bound by
CPI Group (UK) Ltd, Croydon, CR0 4YY

Produced on paper from sustainable forests

In memory of
Michael Green
(1930–2019)

Contents

Introduction   1

1 Big pictures: why meaning matters   3
Dawkins's big picture: universal Darwinism   4
Lewis's big picture: mere Christianity   7
Reflecting on Dawkins and Lewis   11

2 Reasoned belief: faith, proof and evidence   16
C. S. Lewis: fitting things in   17
Richard Dawkins: science and evidence   21
Reflecting on Dawkins and Lewis   24

3 Is there a God?   31
Dawkins: God as an unevidenced delusion   32
C. S. Lewis: God as the heart's desire   35
Reflecting on Dawkins and Lewis   39

4 Human nature: who are we?   44
Dawkins: dancing to the music of DNA   45
Lewis: longing for a true homeland   48
Reflecting on Dawkins and Lewis   51

Conclusion: searching for meaning   55

Notes   59

For further reading   68

Introduction

Why do we find discussions so much more interesting than debates? Perhaps it's because we feel that our own ideas might be helped along by listening to and exploring different perspectives – especially if we're dealing with the really big questions of human existence, such as the meaning of life, the place of science or the existence of God. I love listening to these conversations. And I know others do as well.

This book imagines an interplay of ideas that sadly never took place. What, I have often wondered, would happen if we put two iconic Oxford figures together – the scientific popularizer and celebrity atheist Richard Dawkins on the one hand, and the literary scholar and Christian apologist C. S. Lewis on the other? What could we learn by comparing and contrasting their ideas? How might they help us think through some of life's big questions, such as what life is all about?

Dawkins is an evolutionary biologist who moved from a somewhat nominal Anglicanism to a committed atheism; Lewis is a literary scholar who moved from atheism to what he styled 'mere Christianity' – a form of Christianity that downplayed its denominational aspects. Both are gifted writers, with an enviable capacity for communication, especially in making difficult ideas easy to grasp. And both were leading Oxford academics in their day, perhaps making it appropriate for me – another Oxford academic! – to reflect on their ideas. I have read both these writers in some depth over the years and learned much from engaging with them.[1]

Perhaps Dawkins's reputation has taken a battering recently, given his habit of making outspoken and unwise comments on social media about women and Islam. In a post with the revealing title 'The Sad Unraveling of Richard Dawkins', Salon. com portrayed him as a once-lauded scientist and atheist who shows why ageing intellectuals shouldn't mess around with social media.[2] Yet the big questions about life remain on the table, and Dawkins's high visibility makes him an obvious dialogue partner for our purposes.

This short book can only touch on some of the questions raised by Dawkins and Lewis about these grand debates concerning our place and purpose in our world. I am painfully aware that I will only scratch the surface of some great discussions and debates. However, I hope that this brief engagement with the issues will stimulate my readers to explore them further.

So what might we learn by engaging with both Dawkins and Lewis on some big questions in life, including issues of meaning and faith? About the relationship of the natural sciences and the arts? Or about how best to live in this complex world? I have my own views on these matters, yet my role in this book is to allow both Dawkins and Lewis to be heard, and to stimulate your reflection and discussion. They're both interesting and engaging writers. So I will be standing back and letting them speak for themselves, offering comments and reflection from my own perspective or in the light of my specialist field of science and religion – now firmly established as a major academic discipline at Oxford University and elsewhere. I've learned a lot from engaging with both writers – and I hope you will too.

1

Big pictures: why meaning matters

The term 'big questions' is widely used to refer to ways of thinking about ourselves and our world that help us make sense of things. Psychologists tell us this thinking is natural and that it helps us cope with the pressures and riddles of life.[1] Many now use the term 'big picture' to refer to ways of seeing the world that allow us to engage with life's big questions. It's about a way of seeing that brings things into focus and helps us answer our deepest questions and concerns. Some of these big pictures are religious, some are not. Christianity is a good example of a faith that both tries to make sense of our lives and shows how they can be transformed and renewed. Marxism is a good example of a non-religious – many would say *anti*-religious – world view that aims to explain our world and how it can be changed.

So what is it about human beings that makes us so interested in these big questions? Although lots of answers have been given, nobody really knows. It just seems to be something built into our nature. As the novelist Jeanette Winterson once remarked: 'We cannot simply eat, sleep, hunt and reproduce – we are meaning-seeking creatures.'[2] Some think the answer might lie in our evolutionary past. Others suggest that we have some kind of homing instinct for God as our creator, which makes us search for signs of transcendence or significance. Yet whatever explanation we offer, there's little doubt about how important this sense of meaning can be. The German philosopher Friedrich Nietzsche famously quipped that people can cope with most things if they believe they can see meaning within them.[3]

Meaning is often linked with 'world views' – big pictures of reality that link individual aspects of life together into an interconnected whole. Religious belief is widely acknowledged as affirming the intelligibility and coherence of our world. The philosopher Keith Yandell suggests that a religion is a 'conceptual system that provides an interpretation of the world and the place of human beings in it'.[4] These world views act like lenses, allowing us to see our world and ourselves more clearly by bringing things into focus. Yet some of these world views are non-religious or even anti-religious, as in the case of the two major secular ones of our age: Marxism and Darwinism.

Some have concerns about such world views or big pictures, arguing that they are intellectually overambitious and that we need to content ourselves with partial insights into life. Others go further and suggest that there is no meaning to be found in the first place. If we accept a naturalist world view, it seems to follow that we cannot find any justification of our fundamental beliefs about meaning and values from the nature of the world.[5] And that means we have to create or invent a meaning that is not intrinsic to the world. We'll look at these concerns later, but first we need to turn to our two dialogue partners. What big pictures lie behind their quite divergent outlooks on life?

Dawkins's big picture: universal Darwinism

Dawkins uses the term 'Darwinism' to designate both Darwin's theory of the origins of biological diversity (which like any scientific theory is provisional and open to continual revision and redirection) and a broader world view based on this theory. He introduced the term 'Universal Darwinism' in 1983 to refer to an expanded vision of Darwinism, which he subsequently developed beyond the realm of biology to include explanations of cultural phenomena, including religious belief and the question of purpose in life.[6] Dawkins's *The God Delusion* (2006) developed the suggestion that religion is an 'accidental by-product' of the evolutionary process, a 'misfiring of something useful'.[7] He also uses the metaphysical framework of this Universal Darwinism to reject any notion of purpose – a view summarized in his well-known statement that the universe has 'no design, no purpose, no evil and no good, nothing but blind pitiless indifference'.[8]

Dawkins sees in Darwinism a framework that offers a superior explanation of our universe compared to its potential rivals – such as any form of religious belief. He recalls that while he was at Oundle School, near Peterborough, from 1954 to 1959, he 'retained a strong belief in some sort of unspecified creator', being 'impressed by the beauty and apparent design of the living world'.[9]

Dawkins attributes his loss of any religious faith to two factors. The first was his growing realization that 'Darwin provided the magnificently powerful alternative to biological design which we now know to be true.'[10] This is a recurrent theme in Dawkins's later writings: Darwinism offers an explanation of what is observed in the biological world that is superior to belief in a creator God. The second factor is his belief that there is an 'elementary fallacy' within any argument from design, in that 'any god capable of designing the universe would have needed a fair bit of designing himself'.[11] Darwin's idea of gradual complexification from a 'primeval simplicity' seemed to make a lot more sense to him.

We see here an important idea, namely that you judge a scientific theory or a world view by their ability to make sense of things. Yet Darwinism doesn't – and can't – explain everything. It deals with how life *evolves*. Some of the most significant events in the history of the universe – such as the Big Bang and the origins of life – thus lie beyond its scope. Nonetheless, Dawkins sees in Darwinism a framework for reflecting on human meaning in general and not simply on biological development. He set his ideas out clearly in a short radio talk in 2003:

> [We should] rejoice in the amazing privilege we enjoy. We have been born, and we are going to die. But before we die we have time to understand why we were ever born in the first place. Time to understand the universe into which we have been born. And with that understanding, we finally grow up and realise that there is no help for us outside our own efforts.[12]

Dawkins's Universal Darwinism is to be seen as part of his more general outlook, which treats the natural sciences as the only source of reliable knowledge. This approach, widely adopted within the New Atheist movement, is often termed 'scientism' (a contracted form of 'scientific imperialism'). Although nobody seems able to agree exactly what scientism is, most of its critics tend to see it as a totalizing attitude that regards science as the ultimate judge and ground of all interesting and important questions.[13] Dawkins treats the natural sciences as culturally and intellectually privileged, and regards other disciplines' claims to answer life's great questions as inferior.

The Moral Landscape, a book by the New Atheist writer Sam Harris, is perhaps the stand-out manifesto for scientism, arguing that science is able to determine human moral values – in effect, putting moral philosophy out of business. However, moral philosophers have dismissed Harris's overstatements: it's not exactly difficult to point out that he has merely co-opted a position within moral philosophy, namely a form of utilitarianism that holds that the 'good' is defined in terms of the greatest happiness of the greatest number.[14]

That's one of the reasons why it's so interesting to engage with Dawkins. It forces us to think about the place of science in developing a big picture of life. Can science answer all our big questions about the meaning of life? Or does it really deal with the quite different question of how the universe and human beings *function*? For Dawkins, science tells us all we can hope to know; for others, it has limits that are to be respected, so that we look to other intellectual disciplines or undertakings to answer other questions – including questions of meaning.

The noted biologist John Maynard Smith, for example, declares that scientific theories have nothing to say 'about the value of human beings' – or indeed about moral values in general. For Maynard, biological theories 'say nothing about what is right but only about what is possible', leading us to draw the conclusion that 'we need some other source of values'.[15] A similar view is associated with the biologist Sir Peter Medawar, who shared the Nobel Prize in Physiology or Medicine in 1960 for his part in the discovery of acquired immunological tolerance.[16] Medawar noted the importance of moral and existential questions 'that science cannot answer, and that no conceivable advance of science would empower it to answer'.

Clearly there is more that needs to be said about Dawkins's approach, and we shall pick this up later. But we now need to introduce our second dialogue partner – C. S. Lewis.

Lewis's big picture: mere Christianity

As a teenager, growing up in the Irish city of Belfast, Lewis was convinced that atheism was the only option for a modern intelligent person. Religion had been superseded by science, and in any case consisted of outdated and contradictory myths. Lewis's atheism was hardened by his experience as a soldier in the British Army during the First World War. How could God allow such pointless suffering and devastation? Although Lewis was aware that there were some logical flaws with being angry with a non-existent God, he saw atheism as the default position of any right-thinking person.

During the 1920s, however, Lewis changed his mind. Although he remained convinced that atheism was probably his best option, he found it intellectually uninteresting and came to see it as stifling the life of the imagination. The world of the logically provable was inadequate and unsatisfying: he became convinced that there had to be more to life. He set out this view by contrasting two forces that seemed to be at war within his soul: a plausible yet dull rationalism and a risky yet potentially exhilarating faith.

> On the one side, a many-islanded sea of poetry and myth; on the other, a glib and shallow rationalism. Nearly all that I loved I believed to be imaginary; nearly all that I believed to be real I thought grim and meaningless.[17]

These lines of thought provoked Lewis to reconsider the rationality of belief in God, and eventually to embrace Christianity.

As an atheist who became a Christian, Lewis came to see himself as an apologist for the Christian faith. However, he was always clear that rather than defending any particular kind or style of Christianity, such as Anglicanism or Methodism, he was commending a basic consensual Christian orthodoxy – what he termed 'mere Christianity': 'You will not learn from me', he informed his readers, 'whether you ought to become an Anglican, a Methodist, a Presbyterian, or a Roman Catholic.'[18] Though Lewis did not wish to support any specific Christian institutions, he sought to defend and affirm the basic ideas on which ultimately they were based. His ideas have acquired a new resonance in an age that has come to distrust institutions, not least their instinct to defend themselves rather than the values and ideas they claim to represent.

Yet Lewis was not suggesting that his readers should avoid individual Christian denominations, such as his own Church of England. Nor was he suggesting that the Christian life was to be seen as individualist, without any sense of attachment to or involvement in a Christian community. Rather, each such denomination was to be seen as a distinct embodiment or manifestation of something more fundamental – mere Christianity:

> [Mere Christianity is] like a hall out of which doors open into several rooms. If I can bring anyone into that hall I shall have done what I attempted. But it is in the rooms, not in the hall, that there are fires and chairs and meals. The hall is a place to wait in, a place from which to try the various doors, not a place to live in.[19]

Lewis, then, sees this generous consensual Christian orthodoxy as a spacious hall within which all Christians belong. Yet he notes that Christians actually live out their lives of faith in the rooms in which 'there are fires and chairs and meals'. The Christian life is not about standing around in a hall; it is about sitting down in a place of warmth, hospitality and nourishment – which is what a Christian church ought to be.

Although Lewis regarded Christianity as having many intellectual merits, it is clear that he was especially drawn to its capacity to make sense of his own experiences and intuitions, and of the world he observed around him. He thus came to see God as both the ground of the rationality of the world, and the one who enables us to grasp that rationality. For Lewis, the truths of the Christian faith lie beyond the reach of human reason; yet when those truths are presented and grasped, their rationality can easily be discerned. And one hallmark of that rationality is the ability of the Christian faith to make things intelligible. This basic belief is set out with particular clarity in what has come to be one of his best-known maxims: 'I believe in Christianity as I believe that the Sun has risen, not only because I see it but because by it I see everything else.'[20]

So why would anyone think of Christianity as being a world view? Surely Lewis's concern is a distraction from other more important matters, such as ethics and spirituality? Some would argue that Christianity is fundamentally about salvation, and the transformation of the lives of individuals and communities. This point needs to be taken very seriously. Yet it cannot be overlooked that part of this transformation is the emergence of a new way of thinking about the world – of seeing our universe and our place within it.[21] We might think of Paul's great injunction to his readers to be actively 'transformed by the renewal of your minds' rather than passively 'conformed to this world' (Romans 12.2, NRSV), or his concept of the 'mind of Christ'.[22] And as an atheist turned Christian, Lewis was convinced of the apologetic need to set out the intellectual and imaginative appeal of Christianity to our wider culture[23] – something that required intelligent reflection on the content and practice of faith.

Lewis stands in a long tradition of Christian writers who have highlighted the capacity of Christianity to illuminate reality and help us understand what life is all about. That doesn't mean Lewis reduces Christianity to some kind of pointless intellectual sideline, or that he sees it as an academic diversion from more important things. His point is that an informed understanding of Christianity provides both clarification of what we ought to be doing and a motivation to do it. As Lewis argued in his discussion of the 'Christian hope', what might be seen by some as theological escapism actually turns out to be empowering: 'The Christians who did most for the present world were just those who thought most of the next.'[24]

Reflecting on Dawkins and Lewis

There is growing interest in using the term 'world view' to refer to any attempt, whether religious or secular, to make sense of life's big questions – such as the meaning of life or how we should live.[25] So what questions does this brief engagement with Dawkins and Lewis raise about the importance of world views?

Dawkins and Lewis both see intellectual reflection on such big questions as natural and significant. Both insist that their beliefs – atheism and Christianity respectively – demand and deserve intellectual seriousness and are capable of being developed into larger systems. I agree with them both on the importance of critical and constructive reflection on our beliefs, and regularly commend such a 'discipleship of the mind' to my Christian readers.[26] But are there risks in taking these world views too seriously?

One obvious concern was raised by the philosopher Iris Murdoch, who rightly noted the 'calming whole-making tendencies of human thought',[27] yet believed the human quest for a unified view of nature might lead us to overstate its underlying coherence. Surely we ought to learn to live with the fuzziness of our world and cope with its ambiguities? Another concern is raised by intellectual historians, such as Isaiah Berlin, who point out that world views can create a sense of exclusivism – our view is *right*, so everyone else's is wrong. This easily leads to the demonization of outsiders as intellectually inferior, politically dangerous, culturally alien or simply mentally ill. Such religious or political fundamentalisms are intolerant of dissent within their ranks and of the recognition of intellectual or moral virtues beyond their own spheres.

One of the best discussions of this point comes from the writer Salman Rushdie, who is highly critical of 'any ideology that claims to have a complete, totalized explanation of the world'.[28] Both science and religion can easily become ideologies – above all when they assert that they alone have a monopoly of truth. I see this problem in some religious traditions within and beyond Christianity, just as I also see it in the New Atheism. A world view can very easily become a controlling ideology, enforced by those with vested interests in its preservation.

Linked with this is the danger of being imprisoned within such a world view, failing to realize that there are other ways of making sense of the world. Ludwig Wittgenstein's comment that 'a *picture* held us captive'[29] highlights how easily our understanding of our world can be controlled by an 'organizing myth'[30] – a world view or metanarrative that has, whether we realize it or not, come to dominate our perception of our world. This big picture causes us to think that certain ways of interpreting our experience are natural or self-evidently correct, while blinding us to alternative ways of understanding it.

Dawkins illustrates this difficulty particularly well. Like many within the New Atheism, he holds a view of religion determined by the myth of the warfare of science and religion – a view that emerged during the late nineteenth century, for social reasons, but has long been discredited by historical research.[31] So if, as this controlling myth dictates, science and religion must be seen as at war with each other, what does that imply about the many active scientists who are religious believers? This myth has only one answer to give, and I fear it is a rather thin and unsatisfying one: such people are traitors who collaborate with the enemy. This leads Dawkins to suggest that scientists who believe in or contribute to a positive working relationship between science and religion represent the 'Neville Chamberlain' school.[32]

For those readers who do not recognize this somewhat startling historical allusion, Dawkins is referring to the policy of appeasement that the British Prime Minister, Neville

Chamberlain, adopted towards Adolf Hitler in 1938, in the hope of avoiding total war in Europe. The somewhat distasteful analogy seems to imply that scientists who affirm the import-ance of religion are to be stigmatized as 'appeasers', and that religious people are to be compared, equally offensively, to Hitler. This comparison is intellectual nonsense, perhaps the inevitable outcome of seeing the world through the distorting prism of an inadequate world view. There are, of course, other far more intellectually and historically reliable ways of seeing the relation of science and religion.

Lewis also helps us think about the dangers of controlling myths, which lead us to demonize others. Indeed, we know that one of the concerns that led him to have several intellectual hesitations about embracing Christianity was his perception that he would have to abandon his love for the great Nordic and Greek myths. If Christianity was right, then these had to be wrong; yet in his heart of hearts he knew he could not give up on them. Though having grasped something of the intellec-tual depth and resilience of the Christian faith, Lewis held back from commitment, suspicious of the exclusivism he discerned within its Creeds.

He found a persuasive answer to his concerns in a long con-versation with his Oxford colleague J. R. R. Tolkien in September 1931. Tolkien argued that human beings tell stories that are unconsciously patterned on the Christian grand narrative of creation and redemption. For him, one of the great strengths of that narrative was its ability to explain why we tell stories of meaning in the first place. The Christian gospel enfolded and proclaimed 'a story of a larger kind', which embraced what was good, true and beautiful in the great myths of literature, express-ing it as 'a far-off gleam or echo of *evangelium* in the real world'.[33]

Lewis came to see that the story of Christ was a 'true myth' – that is to say, a myth that functions in the same manner as other myths, yet *really happened*. Christianity possessed the literary form of a myth, which for Lewis meant a story with deep imaginative appeal, conveying a set of ideas. Yet there was a critical difference between Nordic myths and the Christian myth: only the latter was *true*.[34] Pagan myths represented an imperfect grasping towards the truth, a goal finally attained in Christianity. They were to be seen as echoes, rumours or anticipations of Christianity, pointing towards this greater vision of reality that brings their partial insights to a transformative completion. Lewis was thus able to use this intellectual framework to place his love for Nordic and Greek myths within a Christian framework.

So where do these thoughts take us? My own view is that we all need a big picture of our universe and ourselves – but that neither science nor Christianity can deliver that larger vision on its own. If I could put it like this: each illuminates part of our life – but not all of it. Science does not tell me how to be a good person; Christianity does not tell me the values of the fundamental constants of nature. Yet both, taken together, offer a larger picture. They need to be allowed to enrich each other.[35]

It seems to me that Dawkins's view of science is shaped by an unnecessary and distorting metaphysical naturalism, as well as a dogged commitment to a discredited myth of the 'warfare' of science and faith, which blind him to the ways a theological framework might illuminate and enrich our appreciation of science. Happily, there are sections of his writing in which he seems to set such dogmatic assumptions to one side and reflect joyfully on science's ability to help us appreciate the beauty and complexity of nature. Lewis, unfortunately, does not engage with science in any detail or depth,[36] so that his readers must develop their own approaches to science based on his general outlook. Yet this is not difficult to do – and turns out to be profoundly worthwhile.

Having reflected a little on Dawkins and Lewis and their different outlooks, let's look at how they can help us think through some of life's more interesting – and important! – questions. Let's move on to consider the question of faith. Can we – and should we – prove our most cherished beliefs? And what happens if we can't?

2

Reasoned belief: faith, proof and evidence

It's often said that we live in a post-truth world in which we just make up our beliefs. We decide what we would like to be true, then live as if it were true – hoping nobody will come along and ask us difficult questions about our reasons for holding these beliefs. Religious people are often accused of 'wish-fulfilment' – a term used by the atheist psychoanalyst Sigmund Freud in the early twentieth century to refer to the need felt by some to console themselves in believing in a non-existent God. Yet atheism can also be seen as a form of wish-fulfilment. Let's look at an example.

The philosopher Thomas Nagel made it clear that his atheism primarily arose from his dislike of the idea of God:

> It isn't just that I don't believe in God, and, naturally, hope that I'm right in my belief. It's that I hope there is no God! I don't want there to be a God; I don't want the universe to be like that.[1]

It's easy to criticize Nagel for allowing his personal hostility towards God or views about the kind of universe he longed for to affect his supposedly objective philosophical analysis. Yet there are countless people who simply make up their beliefs in the light of their tastes and offer retrospective justifications in the hope of preserving their intellectual integrity. Neither Richard

Dawkins nor C. S. Lewis want anything to do with such ways of thinking. Both insist that we base our lives on something that is true and real, not just something that makes us feel good.

The philosopher Bertrand Russell once commented that 'in the modern world the stupid are cocksure while the intelligent are full of doubt'.[2] With the rise of Nazism in Germany in mind, Russell, an atheist, expressed his deep concern about those who used simplistic and bullying rhetoric to assert the supposedly self-evident truth of their own positions, and who depicted others as deluded fools or charlatans. For some, simplicity is a mark of truth; for Russell, it might also be an indication of someone's failure to face up to the limits of human knowledge and the complexity of our world.

How, then, can we show that our beliefs make sense? Can we prove that they're right? Or if we can't prove them, what's the next best thing? These are important questions. Just about all of us hold certain beliefs, be they religious, ethical or political. Is there a God? What is the good life? Nobody is really certain about the answers to these questions but we can still offer good reasons for what we believe. That's the point behind Russell's famous remark about why people ought to study philosophy: it teaches us 'how to live without certainty, and yet without being paralysed by hesitation'.[3]

So how do Lewis and Dawkins help us to think about these questions? Let's begin by looking at Lewis's approach.

C. S. Lewis: fitting things in

During the twentieth century, Lewis was one of the most outspoken defenders of the rationality of the Christian faith. His distinct approach was to argue that a viewpoint derived from the Bible and the Christian tradition was able to offer a more satisfactory explanation of common human experience than its rivals – especially the atheism he had once himself espoused. His main criterion in making this evaluation was the ability of a way of thinking to take in our observations and experiences.

Lewis's apologetic approach generally takes the form of identifying a common human observation or experience, and then showing how it fits, naturally and plausibly, within a Christian way of looking at things.[4] As we saw earlier, he holds that Christianity provides a big picture of reality, an intellectually capacious and imaginatively satisfying way of seeing things, one that helps make sense of what we observe or experience. For example, he argues that the common human experience of a sense of moral obligation is easily and naturally accommodated within a Christian framework. He also maintains that the human sense of longing for something that is really significant, yet proves frustratingly difficult to satisfy, is a clue to humanity's true fulfilment lying with God.

Lewis's way of thinking will be familiar to many scientists, who are used to working with the approach now generally known as 'inference to the best explanation'. This approach recognizes that there are multiple explanations of observations, and suggests some criteria that might help us work out which explanation is to be considered the best.

For Lewis, our experiences and intuitions – for example, concerning morality and desire – are clues that are meant to 'arouse our suspicions' that there is indeed 'something which is directing the universe'. We come to suspect that our moral experience suggests a 'real law which we did not invent, and which we know we ought to obey', in much the same way as our experience of desire is 'a kind of copy, or echo, or mirage' of another place, which is our true homeland. And as we explore this suspicion, we begin to realize that it has considerable imaginative and explanatory potential.[5]

Lewis thus invites his readers into the Christian way of seeing things and to explore how things look when seen from its standpoint – as if to say, 'Try seeing things this way!' If world views or metanarratives can be compared to lenses, which of them brings things into sharpest focus? Clues, taken by themselves, prove nothing; their importance lies rather in their cumulative and contextual force. In other words, the greater the number of clues that can be satisfactorily accommodated by a given view of reality, the more reliable that view of reality is likely to be.

Lewis here sets out a theme that became increasingly important to him during the 1920s, namely the need for a world view capable of coping with the complexity of our world outside us and our experience within us. While still an atheist, Lewis noted that he found writers such as George Bernard Shaw and H. G. Wells to be 'a little thin' and lacking depth; the 'roughness and density of life' did not seem to be adequately represented in their works. The Christian poet George Herbert, however, seemed to Lewis to excel 'in conveying the very quality of life as we actually live it'; yet instead of 'doing it all directly', he 'insisted on mediating it' through what Lewis then termed 'the Christian mythology'.[6]

This approach to the rationality of religious belief emphasizes its capacity to enfold our experience of the world and help us discern what it means. But some objections need to be considered. For example, Lewis suggests that we judge a set of beliefs by their capacity to make sense of things. But surely we ought to ask what evidence might lead us to adopt those beliefs in the first place, rather than simply taking them as given and then proceeding to evaluate them? It is a perfectly fair point. Yet the issue is more commonplace than might be expected. As Ludwig Wittgenstein pointed out, one and the same proposition or idea may at one point be treated as something *to be tested* and at another as a *rule of testing*.[7]

A more serious concern arises from Lewis's image of Christianity as a sun illuminating an intellectual landscape, so that we can see more clearly and distinctly than we would otherwise. Yet this raises the question of the persistence of shadows – things that don't quite seem to fit into a world view. Lewis himself is quite clear that Christianity does not offer us a totally clear view of reality, and readily concedes that there are certain things that do not fit comfortably – for example, the problem of pain and suffering, the subject of two of his books.[8] His counter-argument would be that we should compare possible approaches and see which makes the most sense of a complex and fuzzy reality. We don't need to – and probably cannot – show that any of them are right; we can, however, show that one seems to make more sense than its rivals, or – to use a more pragmatic approach – that it helps us cope better with the complexities of life.

Lewis himself uses this approach in *Mere Christianity*. He notes that many people have known a 'desire which no experience in this world can satisfy'. After exploring this observation, he offers three possible explanations for such a sense of emptiness and lack of fulfilment. First, this frustration might arise from looking for its true 'object' in the wrong place; we therefore need to keep searching. Second, it might be that there is no true object to be found. If this second explanation is true, there is no point in any further searching, which will only result in repeated disappointment. Lewis, however, suggests there is a third approach, which recognizes that these earthly longings are 'only a kind of copy, or echo, or mirage' of our true homeland. Since this overwhelming desire cannot be fulfilled through anything in the present world, this suggests that its ultimate object lies beyond this world. Lewis concludes that this third is the 'most probable' explanation.[9]

Richard Dawkins: science and evidence

One of the great strengths of the natural sciences is their evidence-based approach to theories. In assessing theories we identify the evidence that needs to be interpreted, and then try to work out which theory is able to make the most sense of it. Think, for example, of Einstein's brilliant theoretical explanation of the photoelectric effect, for which he was awarded the Nobel Prize in Physics in 1921. Dawkins is suspicious of religious beliefs because they seem to involve a retreat from critical thinking and a disengagement from evidence-based reasoning. His commitment to a scientific assessment of evidence leads him to adopt a strongly critical attitude towards any beliefs inadequately grounded in the observable: 'As a lover of truth, I am suspicious of strongly held beliefs that are unsupported by evidence.'[10] For Dawkins, religious faith is 'blind trust, in the absence of evidence, even in the teeth of evidence'.[11]

Dawkins here highlights the importance of proof, evidence and faith in our attempts to make sense of our world and our lives, raising some serious questions about the rationality of religious belief.[12] He is absolutely right to insist on the need for evidential foundations for belief, no matter what form those beliefs might take. In his 1995 'A Prayer for my Daughter', he makes some important points about belief and evidence that are clearly relevant:

> Next time somebody tells you that something is true, why not say to them: 'What kind of evidence is there for that?' And if they can't give you a good answer, I hope you'll think very carefully before you believe a word they say.[13]

Dawkins thus challenges arguments based on tradition or authority. It doesn't matter how important someone is; you judge his or her beliefs on the evidence they are able to adduce in support of them.

He views this robust use of evidence as a critical tool, seen at its best in the practices of the natural sciences. Science is about what can be proved to be true on the basis of evidence. Yet I am not persuaded that Dawkins deals successfully with the obvious dilemma that we so often face as human beings – that is, not having enough evidence to prove a core belief. Scientists regularly have to confront the problem of the 'underdetermination' of theory by evidence.[14] In other words, the evidence is often insufficient to compel us to accept one theory over another, in that each theory has some evidential support.

For Dawkins, there is no room for faith in science, precisely because the evidence compels us to draw certain valid conclusions. In *The Selfish Gene* he proposes an absolute dichotomy between 'blind faith' and 'overwhelming, publicly available evidence':

> But what, after all, is faith? It is a state of mind that leads people to believe something – it doesn't matter what – in the total absence of supporting evidence. If there were good supporting evidence, then faith would be superfluous, for the evidence would compel us to believe it anyway.[15]

I fully concede the importance of 'good supporting evidence' for beliefs and am suspicious of those who resist submitting their beliefs to critical reflection. But I'm not sure it's really as simple as Dawkins suggests.

Why? The issue is that Dawkins here fails to make the critically important distinction between the total absence of supporting evidence and the absence of totally supporting evidence. Consider, for example, the current debate within cosmology over whether the Big Bang gave rise to a single universe or a series of universes (the so-called multiverse).[16] I know distinguished scientists in Oxford who support the former approach and equally distinguished scientists who support the latter. Both are real options for informed and thinking scientists, who make their decisions on the basis of their judgements of how best to interpret the evidence, and who *believe* – but cannot *prove* – that their interpretation is correct. There may be evidence for both beliefs but there is *compelling* evidence for neither. As in this case, scientists often have to make judgements about how best to make sense of evidence supportive of several possible conclusions.

Dawkins overstates the ease with which scientists navigate their way from observations of our universe to theories about it, conveniently overlooking the serious intellectual difficulties raised by the underdetermination of theory by evidence. Yet he is entirely right to highlight the importance of evidence-based thinking in science, and to raise concerns about those who simply demand we accept their ideas, or ask us to ignore evidence or avoid serious thinking about our universe or the meaning of life.

The difficulty is that science doesn't always deliver simple judgements. For example, consider the following question: 'Which is the best approach to quantum theory?' A recent survey of experts in the field showed a wide range of commitments to the ten major interpretations – again showing the importance of personal judgement in these decisions.[17] As these interpretations are inconsistent with one another, this raises some difficult questions for the simplistic 'science proves its beliefs' outlook.

Another point that needs to be noted is that evidence accumulates over time – for example, through the development of new forms of technology that allow us to measure quantities once inaccessible to us, such as the recession speeds of distant galaxies. This leads to some occasionally spectacular changes in scientific thinking. Before the First World War, the dominant scientific understanding of our universe was that it had always existed and changed in only superficial ways over time.[18] Now we believe that the universe came into being about 13.8 billion years ago through the Big Bang. That's a massive change! But it's how science works. It changes its mind as new evidence and better theories develop.

Dawkins often seems to make an illegitimate logical transition from 'this cannot be proved' to 'this is false'. During a 1999 debate entitled 'Is Science Killing the Soul?' a member of the audience asked whether science could offer people consolation similar to that offered by religion – for example, after the death of a close friend or relative. Dawkins's response was puzzling: 'The fact that religion may console you doesn't of course make it true. It's a moot point whether one wishes to be consoled by a falsehood.'[19] He here slides effortlessly from saying that consolation does not make religion true to saying that religion is false. Now while this might seem to be an entirely natural inference for Dawkins, it is not a logically valid conclusion. It does not follow that since *A* has not been proved, *A* is false.

Reflecting on Dawkins and Lewis

Dawkins and Lewis are both really interesting and stimulating thinkers. So how might they help us think through this issue of evidence and faith? I like and respect Dawkins's emphasis on providing good reasons for what we believe, and hope more scientists will pay attention to him. Why, I have often wondered, do so many theoretical physicists love super-string theory, put forward by Edward Witten in 1995, when there is no evidence to support it and it makes absolutely no predictions? Many scientists regard it as pure fantasy and wish that colleagues enamoured of the theory would rediscover their experimental roots.[20] But I also hope that religious believers will take Dawkins's point seriously and show that good reasons can be offered for their belief. Lewis is a good example of a religious thinker who sets out a reasoned case for faith, and he – and others like him – need to be heard in our wider culture.

Lewis, however, is more cautious than Dawkins at this point, emphasizing that philosophical and existential attempts to make sense of our world and our lives lack the precision of mathematics and logic. We have to make judgements about how well our world views fit with what we observe and ex-perience. Lewis does not try to prove the existence of God on a priori grounds. Instead he invites us to see how what we observe in the world around us and experience within us fits the Christian way of seeing things, almost as if we were trying on a hat or coat. He often prefers to use stories rather than arguments to make these points, believing that narratives are a more effective means of communication and exploration of the complexities of life.[21]

So how do Dawkins and Lewis cope with things that don't seem to fit their world views? In Lewis's case the most obvi-ous inconsistency would seem to be the existence of suffer-ing. He was aware of this concern and addressed it in two of his works: *The Problem of Pain* (1940) and *A Grief Observed* (1961).[22] Though his case is not intellectually watertight, there is no doubt that he takes the force of such concerns seriously, leading him to show how an incarnational faith can accommo-date the existence of suffering and even offer a way of coping with its trauma.[23]

In Dawkins's case, the stand-out inconsistency within his scientific atheism is the existence of so many people who be-lieve in a God or gods. While he offers a Darwinian debunking argument against such belief, his dominant strategy – especially in *The God Delusion* – is to assert the idiocy of religious be-lievers, who are dismissed as deluded or perhaps even mentally ill. Believing in God is just like believing in the Tooth Fairy or Santa Claus – an infantile illusion that is abandoned when one grows up, or certainly ought to be. Religious people, however, remain locked within a childish mentality, their intellectual growth stunted and impaired.

I have to confess some concerns about this approach, which frankly struggles to make sense of those who – like myself or Lewis – made the transition from atheism to Christianity *as adults*. However, I am in complete sympathy with Dawkins when he suggests that we ought to prove – or at least provide reasons for – what we believe. Here are three statements I believe to be right, on the basis of the evidence available to me:

1 The annual rainfall in the English city of Durham in 1870 was 604.8 mm.[24]
2 The atomic weight of the only stable isotope of gold is 197.[25]
3 The chemical formula for water is H_2O.[26]

All three of these statements meet the gold standard for reliability in that each is rigorously based on evidence. *Yet none of them seem very important.* A world based on such statements is not merely very small and dull, it is existentially unsatisfying; simply an aggregation of facts. I'm not sure that living in such a mental world would amount to enough, and it certainly wouldn't be meaningful. We need more.

That's why so many people hold social, political, ethical and religious beliefs that go beyond the available evidence but help us work out what is good and how we ought to live. Let's note three examples of influential and important beliefs that cannot be proved true:

1 There is no God.
2 There is a God.
3 Democracy is the best form of government.

Each of these views commands some degree of support in today's complex and multifaceted world. But none of them can be *proved* to be true. If we followed Dawkins's criteria and accepted only those beliefs that can be proved to be right, we would have to turn our backs on all three of these beliefs – and many others drawn from the worlds of religion (and its critics), ethics and politics. But we don't.

Why not? Because we realize that things are a lot more complicated than Dawkins allows. You can prove shallow truths such as $2 + 2 = 4$. But our really deep and significant beliefs lie beyond proof, and we have to learn to live with this. It is interesting to note how often Dawkins's New Atheist colleague Christopher Hitchens makes criticisms of theism that often rest on unproved moral values, which he appears to assume will be shared by his readers and seen as self-evidently correct. Yet these values, like theism itself, turn out to be unproved and unprovable.

This problem is widely recognized. Bertrand Russell, for example, self-defined as an atheist (at least in the popular sense of the word). But he was really an agnostic, who knew that the question of whether God existed could not be proved one way or the other.[27] His atheism was basically a lifestyle choice, a decision to live and act in a certain way, knowing it ultimately involved an act of faith. Dawkins describes this position as 'de facto atheism' and summarizes it as follows: 'I cannot know for certain but I think God is very improbable, and I live my life on the assumption that he is not there.'[28]

The physicist John Polkinghorne likewise points out that no form of human truth-seeking enquiry can achieve absolute certainty about its conclusions. Polkinghorne found Christianity to be intellectually and personally compelling. Yet he was clear that neither science nor religion can ever hope to establish or attain a 'logically coercive proof of the kind that only a fool could deny'.[29] Both enterprises necessarily involve 'some degree of intellectual precariousness', since the 'unavoidable epistemic condition of humanity' is that we commit ourselves to beliefs we have good reason to *accept* as true but cannot *prove* to be true.[30]

Since the publication of *The God Delusion* in 2006, Dawkins seems to have moved away from its simplistic views about truth and to have recognized this dilemma that we face as human beings – that we believe certain things that lie beyond absolute proof but nevertheless believe we are justified in believing them. Dawkins sets out rational and evidential criteria by which he chastises religious beliefs. So why does he not apply those same criteria to his own beliefs? This remarkable rational asymmetry represents a significant vulnerability within the New Atheist movement as a whole and has often been challenged by its critics. Dawkins is haunted by the fear that his own committed form of atheism cannot be sustained in the light of the criteria of rationality he uses in his criticism of religion. These criteria can too easily be turned against him by his critics. Judge yourself by the standards by which you judge others!

Yet at times Dawkins comes close to facing up to this major difficulty with his approach. In a mannerly and thoughtful debate with Rowan Williams, hosted by Oxford University in February 2012,[31] Dawkins was perfectly clear about this point: he could not *prove* there was no God. In a sense, he was therefore an agnostic.

Lewis similarly recognizes the limits placed on the human quest for certainty. He saw God as the best way of making sense of our world and inhabiting it meaningfully. But he also knew this belief could not be proved in the way someone could provide, say, mathematical proofs of Fermat's last theorem.

Happily, this moves us away from facile demands for 'proving' our answers to what the philosopher Karl Popper called 'ultimate questions' – such as the meaning of life. For Popper, these questions just couldn't be answered decisively by scientific experimentation or rational arguments. They remain enormously important for human beings and are stubbornly resistant to glib and slick answers.

We need to sound a note of caution here. Religion is often framed solely in terms of beliefs about God, overlooking its equally significant beliefs about the dignity and destiny of human beings. Faith is not simply a set of doctrines about the transcendent but a set of commitments about how we understand and respond to our fellow human beings. Anyway, is religion really just about *ideas*? What about the practices, attitudes and values entangled with religious beliefs? The atheist philosopher Alain de Botton recently suggested that atheists ought to give up on their crudely rationalist accounts of religion, and appreciate how the multiple layers of religious commitment and practice create a sense of community and help people connect effectively with the natural world.[32]

Dawkins and Lewis, in their different ways, help Christians reflect on the nature of faith. Dawkins often overstates his concerns, and by doing so limits his appeal to the more uncritical fringes of atheism. Faith, he suggests, is: 'blind trust, in the absence of evidence, even in the teeth of evidence';[33] a 'process of non-thinking'; 'evil precisely because it requires no justification, and brooks no argument'.[34] I cannot help but feel that Dawkins really ought to read more Christian writers before making such muddled overstatements about something he does not understand, a habit he has unfortunately returned to more recently in a series of outrageous – and rightly ridiculed – Twitter postings about women and Muslims.

Lewis has concerns as well. One of the more important relates to an over-emphasis on rational arguments for faith. As a result, some Christians are preoccupied with showing the truth of their faith, often echoing the 'glib and shallow rationalism'[35] of their critics, and thus fail to bring out its important emphasis on meaning and its capacity to transform life. Lewis holds that stories are a far better way both to explore the reasonableness of the Christian faith and challenge the adequacy of its rivals, and to express Christianity's capacity to transform life.[36] Faith is not about evading human reason; it is about recognizing and transcending its limits rather than remaining trapped within the austere 'iron cage' of rationalism (to use Max Weber's famous term).

Perhaps the biggest question that separates Dawkins and Lewis is whether there is a God. In the next chapter we shall reflect on this important debate and consider what may be learned from it.

3

Is there a God?

Popular debates are great fun. For a start, they cut out scholarship and serious arguments, and focus on ridiculing your opponent rather than taking her ideas seriously. One of the things I so much enjoyed in debate with Christopher Hitchens was his ability to deploy brilliant rhetorical flourishes, dismissing religious and other people he didn't like with a panache I could never hope to match. After listening to Hitchens, I began to realize that Aristotle was right: nothing convinces like conviction.[1] There's a lesson in that for public speakers: if you're weak on evidence, make sure you're strong on rhetoric.

Yet most of us know that we can't rest content with such superficial engagement with life's big questions, no matter how much we may enjoy it. Debating is an amusing form of entertainment; sadly, it hardly ever solves the big questions of life. Scholarship complexifies things, showing that they're not as simple as some religious and secular propagandists would wish. So let's reflect on the question of God, allowing Dawkins and Lewis to help us think this through.

First, we need to be clear that 'being religious' and 'believing in God' are not the same. Serious scholarship rejects simplistic definitions that equate religion with belief in a God or gods, a view found throughout the New Atheist movement – for example, in Daniel Dennett's bizarre statement that 'a religion without God or gods is like a vertebrate without a backbone'.[2] Any serious student of religion knows that Buddhism – one of the world's major faiths – lacks any such core belief. Scholars have chided New Atheist writers such as Dennett for simply acquiescing 'in a set of common-sense assumptions about religion that circulate in the American context'.[3]

Nobody seems to have come up with a definition of 'religion' that really works. It's not difficult to work out why. 'Religion' is a 'false universal', a European construct that worked better as a political and ideological tool than as a scientific or scholarly concept.[4] For this reason I shall focus simply on belief in God. How reasonable is this? Both Dawkins and Lewis give this question extended discussion, so let's look at some of the points they make, and see how these help us reflect on the issues involved.

Dawkins: God as an unevidenced delusion

Dawkins takes the view that God is a good – perhaps the best – example of an unevidenced belief; a delusion. People believe in God because this belief has been hammered into them by aggressively religious families or schools, or because they have failed to think seriously about superior scientific understandings of the world, which make belief in God both unnecessary and implausible. No good reason can be given for believing in God. It is irrational for a modern person to believe in God, which must be seen as a throwback to an earlier pre-scientific age in which such beliefs seemed credible.[5]

These are important arguments. Dawkins is critical of those who invoke an unobserved and unobservable entity – such as God – to explain what we see around us in the world. It's a fair point. Science has gained its reputation as an outstanding means of making sense of our world for many reasons, including its scepticism about going beyond what may be observed. Yet while science aims to 'preserve the phenomena', it often turns out that explaining those observations involves postulating unobserved and unobservable entities, such as dark matter.

We might also consider Newton's idea of gravity. Few now have the slightest difficulty with this notion, yet when proposed back in the seventeenth century it was seen as a shocking idea – precisely because it could be neither observed nor experienced by any human sensory organ. Newton was clear that while gravity could not be observed, it made sense of what was observed. It was a legitimate scientific inference from an observable phenomenon to the unobservable entity that best explains it.[6]

Christians take the view that believing in God helps us make sense of the world, offering a larger framework or big picture into which fits what we observe and experience. Dawkins argues that this involves adding an unobserved and intrinsically complicated entity – God – to the inventory of the universe. Science is about keeping things as simple as possible – which is one reason why Dawkins prefers atheism to Christianity. It seems a simpler and neater idea.

Now this is a fair point. Suppose I was asked to decide which of several possible scientific explanations of an observation was the best. One criterion often used is that of simplicity. The philosopher Richard Swinburne focuses on this and argues that theism is the most elegant and simple explanation of our world.[7] Some atheists argue that it's easier to believe in no God than in one God. Yet although some philosophers of science have argued that the simplest theory is always the best, the history of science just doesn't bear this out.[8]

As we noted, Dawkins's emphasis on the intellectual simplicity of atheism is often framed in terms of Christianity adding one extra – yet totally unnecessary – item to the contents of the universe, namely God. This leads Dawkins to emphasize the superior conceptual parsimony of atheism on the one hand, and to demand proof for the existence of this God on the other. Yet Christians do not see God as a physical object within the universe, analogous to a new moon orbiting the planet Neptune. God is rather the ground and cause of all things, who stands behind and beyond the universe, while also choosing to self-disclose in human form. As William Inge (1860–1954), a former Lady Margaret Professor of Divinity at Cambridge University, pointed out, rationalists try to 'find a place for God' in the world. Christians, however, think of God not as part of a painting or diagram but rather as 'the canvas on which the picture is painted, or the frame in which it is set'.[9]

Dawkins, however, has another point to make that needs to be taken very seriously, namely the moral character of God. God, for Dawkins, is intellectually superfluous and morally repugnant. God is a tyrant, an oppressor who imprisons humanity within a constricted and constraining intellectual straitjacket. *The God Delusion* speaks eloquently of a 'nasty god' who 'stalks every page of the Old Testament'.[10] Some might see this as a prejudicial stereotyping of Judaism; others, however, would see Dawkins's focus on the Old Testament as a necessary tactic to discredit any form of monotheism, given the New Testament's rather attractive emphasis on divine love and compassion.

Scholars of the Old Testament fault Dawkins for his wooden and uncomprehending reading of this text, particularly his failure to do justice to the complexity of its vision of God,[11] or to realize that Christians interpret the Old Testament in the light of Jesus Christ, seen as the fulfilment of Law and prophets (Matthew 5.17). This is one of the reasons why so many have criticized Dawkins and others within the New Atheism for ridiculing and vilifying a concept of God that seems to bear little relation to the Christian God – an idealized (or demonized?)

invention designed with the needs of atheist apologetics in mind, playing on dark cultural suspicions of religion and exploiting a diminishing general knowledge of Christian beliefs and practices.

Dawkins, then, raises some important questions. Let's bring C. S. Lewis into the conversation and see what issues he opens up for us.

C. S. Lewis: *God as the heart's desire*

We have already noted that as a teenager, Lewis considered atheism the self-evident position of any thinking person. Yet over a period of about ten years he began to entertain doubts, increasingly seeing this way of thinking as imaginatively and emotionally impoverished. His experience of the brutality and apparent pointlessness of the First World War initially confirmed his atheism; further reflection suggested it was not so straightforward:

> My argument against God was that the universe seemed so cruel and unjust. But how had I got this idea of just and unjust? A man does not call a line crooked unless he has some idea of a straight line. What was I comparing this universe with when I called it unjust? . . . In the very act of trying to prove that God did not exist – in other words, that the whole of reality was senseless – I found I was forced to assume that one part of reality – namely my idea of justice – was full of sense.[12]

Lewis's transition from atheism to Christianity proceeded in stages. Initially he realized that the concept of God offered both an explanation and a confirmation of human moral values. Yet this essentially philosophical idea of God gave way to the notion of God as a living reality – someone we could know, not just know *about*. Lewis thus came to see God as the source and goal of human longing. His grounds for believing in God were not that this would make him a happier human being but because the Christian vision of God was true and trustworthy and brought joy and fulfilment in its wake.

For Lewis, belief in God was neither a distraction from life nor a spurious means of finding consolation. Discovering God was about discovering his own true identity and recalibrating his reason and imagination in the light of this new way of seeing himself and the world. God is neither an object within our universe nor a mere abstract philosophical idea. Although our quest may begin with rational arguments or take these in along the way, the goal of that quest is a personal reality:

> [The existence of God] is a speculative question as long as it is a question at all. But once it has been answered in the affirmative, you get quite a new situation . . . You are no longer faced with an argument which demands your assent, but with a Person who demands your confidence.[13]

The point Lewis is making is that religious belief is grounded on rational norms that are not the same as those governing scientific theories. The former are governed by the 'logic of personal relations', the latter by the 'logic of speculative thought'.

For Lewis, God is 'a dynamic, pulsating activity, a life, almost a kind of drama. Almost, if you will not think me irreverent, a kind of dance.'[14] To have faith in God is not primarily to give intellectual assent to an idea about God but to step into a greater picture of our world and become part of it. 'Each of us has got to enter that pattern, take his place in that dance. There is no other way to the happiness for which we are made.'[15] Belief in God is not about assenting to theological propositions but about stepping into a story – an idea Lewis developed in detail in *The Chronicles of Narnia* – or taking part in God's dance. It is about entering into a new world and inhabiting it meaningfully. Theology is the outcome – not the precondition – of reflective inhabitation of this new way of seeing ourselves and our world.[16]

So which God are we talking about? Lewis is quite clear about this: it is the God made known and available through Jesus Christ, whose significance is to be grasped through both reason and the imagination. Belief in this God allows us to make sense of our world, so that we see it truly; yet it is also about the discernment of what we and our universe mean and how this informs the way we live. For Lewis, 'reason is the natural organ of truth; but imagination is the organ of meaning'.[17] As he noted in an important essay on Dante's vision of the Christian faith, we are thus enabled to 'not only understand the doctrine but see the picture'.[18]

Like a scientist, Lewis aimed to evaluate the reliability of his beliefs by checking them out against observations. This helps us understand why he called himself an 'empirical theist': he assessed Christianity – especially its understanding of God – by asking how well this 'fits in' with what he experienced. Readers of *Mere Christianity* will be familiar with his reflections on the human sense of moral responsibility, and the deep and elusive sense of yearning – which he termed 'joy' – that was such an integral part of his world of experience.

Yet Lewis's approach to belief in God raises questions. One of the most obvious is this: he does not establish the existence of God by evidence-based reasoning. His approach seems rather to be assessing the Christian idea of God by seeing how well it makes sense of experience. Surely he should prove the existence of God on the basis of the evidence?

It's an important question – but not easily answered. Wittgenstein, as we noted in Chapter 2, pointed out that the complexities of human reasoning processes are such that one and the same proposition or idea may at one point be treated as something *to be tested* and at another as a *rule of testing*.[19] Lewis seems to have adopted a binary solution during the late 1920s: either a recovery of belief in God or a confirmation and consolidation of his atheism. His was thus a *comparative* judgement, in which he set two already familiar positions side by side, considering how well they 'conveyed' or rendered actual human experience.

It's interesting to set Lewis alongside Dawkins at this point. In Chapter 1 we noted Dawkins's view that the universe has neither design nor purpose. We need to look at this passage more closely and note the method he uses in drawing this conclusion: 'The universe we observe has precisely the properties we should expect if there is, at bottom, no design, no purpose, no evil and no good, nothing but blind pitiless indifference.'[20] Dawkins here argues that there is a congruence or convergence of our actual observations of the universe and what we would expect if it is devoid of any intrinsic purpose, meaning or value.

Although Dawkins and Lewis reach quite different conclusions, their lines of argument are surprisingly similar. Each is asking which way of thinking seems to fit in better with our observations. The question is resonance or consonance between theory and observation, not proof of theory by observation. In the end, these two thinkers reach different *judgements* about God, yet by similar intellectual trajectories; neither of their positions is proved or provable. Sometimes the best theory is complicated and needs to be judged by its empirical adequacy – in other words, its ability to make sense of what we observe and experience. That's one of the main reasons why I moved away from atheism to Christianity. It seemed to me that atheism didn't really help me make sense of the complexities of our world or human experience, whereas Christianity did.

Reflecting on Dawkins and Lewis

So what can be learned from these two thinkers who take such radically different perspectives on belief in God? Perhaps one obvious conclusion is that both Dawkins and Lewis are men of faith, in that both hold committed positions that cannot be proved right but which they clearly regard as justified and reasonable. We have to learn to live with a degree of rational uncertainty about our deepest beliefs and values. In Chapter 2 we noted Bertrand Russell's remark that philosophy teaches us 'how to live without certainty, and yet without being paralysed by hesitation'.[21] A similar view was taken by the philosopher of science Michael Polanyi: 'There is no finished certainty to our knowledge, but there is no sceptical despair either. Through all our different kinds of knowledge, there is reasonable faith, personal responsibility, and continuing hope.'[22]

To his critics, Dawkins's views on faith and proof seem to be philosophically thin and emotionally inadequate, characterized by a narrow, limited account of the capacity of human beings to know what really matters and live out their lives on its basis. It is instructive to compare Dawkins's shallow account of proof with the more reflective and realistic reflections of poets such as Alfred, Lord Tennyson.[23] His 1885 poem 'The Ancient Sage' provides a succinct summary of the dilemma of human beings as they try to make sense of our world and live meaningfully within it:

> For nothing worthy proving can be proven,
> Nor yet disproven.[24]

A decision to live on the basis of one of the many atheist or theistic outlooks requires going beyond the demonstrable certainties of logic or the secure findings of the natural sciences. The philosopher John Gray remarked that 'if you want to understand atheism and religion, you must forget the popular notion that they are opposites'.[25] In terms of their intellectual precariousness, both atheism and Christianity reflect the epistemic limits of human beings, who show a tendency to want to believe more – whether that belief is religious or secular – than the evidence actually warrants. The psychologist Fraser Watts points this out in a perceptive and constructive way:

> There is nothing unique to religion about people holding views or beliefs with some rational basis, but no compelling argument. Indeed, the comment I would make from a psychological perspective is that this is the norm in human cognition, not the exception; it is not specific to religion.[26]

I find that setting Lewis and Dawkins side by side illuminates both the human condition and the inevitability of some form of faith in living a meaningful life. Yet many would suggest that the existence of suffering calls into question whether life can be said to be 'meaningful' in any sense of the word. As we noted earlier, this was certainly the view Lewis took during the early 1920s. He fought in the British Army during the First World War and was appalled by the destruction and brutality he witnessed.[27] Although his ambition to join the ranks of Britain's 'war poets' never came to anything, his poetry of this period makes it clear he was angry with God for allowing such devastation (even though he did not actually believe there was a God for him to be angry with). His 1918 poem 'Ode for New Year's Day', written under fire near the French town of Arras in January 1918, proclaims the final death of a callous and indifferent God who was a human invention in the first place. This raises an intriguing question: was Lewis's early atheism the result of his revulsion against a specific concept of God that he felt morally unable to accept?

A similar theme is found in Dawkins's *The God Delusion*. Although Dawkins clearly believes there is no intellectual case for the existence of any kind of God, he is severely critical of the moral character of the God of the Old Testament – the Hebrew Bible:

> The God of the Old Testament is arguably the most unpleasant character in all fiction: jealous and proud of it; a petty, unjust, unforgiving control-freak; a vindictive, bloodthirsty ethnic cleanser; a misogynistic, homophobic, racist, infanticidal, genocidal, filicidal, pestilential, megalomaniacal, sadomasochistic, capriciously malevolent bully.[28]

This disturbing outpouring of contempt and vilification is illuminating, for it indicates that we cannot separate the question of 'belief in God' from that of 'What God are we talking about?'

Yet this outburst raises a very significant difficulty that goes beyond its obvious prejudicial stereotyping and simplistic misrepresentations. Dawkins is clear there is no God. The God of the Old Testament is therefore a human invention, a fabrication that reflects the agendas and prejudices of human beings. Christopher Hitchens, Dawkins's fellow New Atheist, points out that from an atheist perspective, human beings create a God who is like them: 'God did not create man in his own image. Evidently, it was the other way about.'[29] Both God and religions must be recognized as 'man-made'.[30] Human religion illuminates human nature.

This issue is central to the writings of the German atheist philosopher Ludwig Feuerbach, who influenced both Karl Marx and Sigmund Freud. In his *Essence of Christianity* (1841), Feuerbach argued that human beings invent gods – and in so doing disclose their true natures, aspirations and fears.

The study of religion thus offers a way of understanding human nature.[31]

So if, as Dawkins asserts, God is a 'bloodthirsty ethnic cleanser', what does that say about the people who invented this God? Dawkins doesn't seem to have grasped the significance of this question. Happily, others have – such as the philosopher Bernard Williams. Although Williams shared Dawkins's intense distaste for religion, he was acutely aware of the intellectual implications of any suggestion that religion was intrinsically evil. Williams had read Feuerbach's atheist manifesto of the 1840s and knew that if there is no God, then religion can only mirror the heart and soul of human beings, who are thus exposed as the creators of such (allegedly) horrific and repulsive values:

> For granted that [religion's] transcendental claim is false, human beings must have dreamed it, and we need an understanding of why this was the content of their dream. (Humanism – in the contemporary sense of a secularist and anti-religious movement – seems seldom to have faced fully a very immediate consequence of its own views: that this terrible thing, religion, is a *human* creation.)[32]

Within an atheist perspective, a repulsive deity is the mirror image of the repulsive human beings who invented this idea of God. So what does this tell us about human nature? Given the human moral fiascos of the twentieth century, few would now echo the naive moral optimism of the Victorian atheist poet Algernon Charles Swinburne: 'Glory to Man in the highest! for Man is the master of things.'[33] The sheer irrationality of the two total wars of the twentieth century reduced many – such as Bertrand Russell – to despair:

> Man is a rational animal – so at least I have been told. Throughout a long life, I have looked diligently for

evidence in favor of this statement, but so far I have not had the good fortune to come across it.[34]

These lines of thought move us away from the question of God to the perhaps more troubling one of human nature. Why troubling? Because any good theory of human nature is like a mirror: it shows us how we really are rather than how we would like to be. So what insights do Lewis and Dawkins offer on this issue?

4

Human nature: who are we?

Who are we? We tend to identify ourselves in a number of ways. As the Harvard economist Amartya Sen points out: 'identities are robustly plural'.[1] We might define ourselves using a range of markers – such as ethnicity, nationality, gender or sexuality – while still seeing ourselves as single individuals each with a distinct identity. Sociologists suggest that we define ourselves in terms of multiple narratives, informing different aspects of our existence – for example, a Christian narrative provides a religious mooring for our existence, but is supplemented by various cultural, social and political narratives. Each of us ends up developing our own distinct way of weaving these together,[2] perhaps giving one of them priority in a particular context.

One question that cannot be overlooked is the human tendency to do some very unwise things. We have developed technologies that now put us in a unique position. Unlike any other species, we might be able deliberately to bring about our own mass destruction – perhaps through the reckless use of nuclear weapons or designer pathogens. But why would humanity do something so utterly stupid and perverse as to bring about its own extinction event? Might there be something wrong with us that allows – or even impels – us to do unwise things? The logic of Cold War Rationality, in which the notion of Mutually Assured Destruction played a central role, was famously captured in Stanley Kubrick's 1964 film *Dr. Strangelove or: How I Learned to Stop Worrying and Love the Bomb*.[3]

These questions are never going to go away, and remain a constant worry for those humanists who make humanity 'the measure of all things' (to draw on a theme of the pre-Socratic Greek philosopher Protagoras). If we are both judge and jury of our own values we can easily become locked into potentially delusional or self-serving agendas. We need to be self-critical – to challenge our self-images and reflect on the strengths and weaknesses of human nature. Dawkins and Lewis both do this, though in rather different ways, opening up some fascinating and important questions. Let's begin by looking at some ideas developed in Dawkins's first book, *The Selfish Gene.*

Dawkins: dancing to the music of DNA

I remember reading *The Selfish Gene* when I was researching molecular biophysics at Oxford University back in 1977, a year after it first appeared. It was obvious that Dawkins was a superb scientific popularizer, both synthesizing and explaining George Williams's views on natural selection, William Hamilton's theory of kin selection and Robert Trivers's views on reciprocal altruism. Yet Dawkins did more than explain other people's ideas; he added one of his own, namely the 'meme' as a kind of metaphor for understanding cultural evolution. Perhaps his most significant achievement in *The Selfish Gene* is his synthesis of these ideas to depict human beings as accidental and unintended outcomes of a blind process, whose lives are influenced and directed by genetic forces we do not fully understand and cannot fully control.

In *The Selfish Gene*, Dawkins presents the evolutionary process from the perspective of the gene, believing such a 'gene's eye' approach to be the best way of allowing the coherence of Darwinian evolutionary theory to be grasped imaginatively. The core theme of this approach is summed up in a sentence from his lecture notes of 1966: 'our basic expectation on the basis of the orthodox neo-Darwinian theory of evolution is that *Genes will be "selfish.*"'[4] This idea was developed and given further substance and justification in *The Selfish Gene*: 'A predominant quality to be expected in a successful gene is ruthless selfishness. This gene selfishness will usually give rise to selfishness in individual behaviour.'[5]

On this reading of things, human selfishness is to be seen as an expression of an underlying genetic predisposition over which we have no control. Even altruism, Dawkins argues, can be explained in terms of this paradigm of selfishness, in that it represents a mechanism by which genes are able to ensure their survival overall, even if some gene-bearing individuals have to be sacrificed along the way.

Dawkins is good at crafting phrases that capture our imaginations, memorably summing up his core themes. In his *River out of Eden* – which is a survey of a Darwinian view of life – he argues that we are the unwitting prisoners and tools of our genes. Whether we like it or not, our motivations and actions are shaped by our genetic inheritance – by DNA, which codes and transmits our individual genetic identities: 'DNA neither knows nor cares. DNA just is. And we dance to its music.'[6] As Dawkins himself concedes, this is a somewhat bleak outlook. We cannot break free from our genetic history. Our evolutionary past continues to be a living presence and influence. This naturally raises the question of whether we can sever this entanglement with the past and start all over again.

As we have seen, Dawkins argues that our genetic history predisposes us to act in certain selfish manners. So can we break free from this genetically induced selfishness? Dawkins suggests that he is like an oncologist, whose professional speciality is studying cancer and whose professional vocation is fighting it. Our genes may 'instruct us to be selfish' but we are under no obligation to obey them. The future of humanity depends on our resisting this genetic legacy, not going along with it: 'Let us try to *teach* generosity and altruism, because we are born selfish. Let us understand what our own selfish genes are up to, because we may then at least have the chance to upset their designs.'[7]

Although we are shaped and conditioned by our 'selfish genes', Dawkins argues that we can realize the ways we are trapped by our genes and thus devise strategies for resisting their malign influence. Humanity is trapped in patterns of thought and action ultimately not of its own choosing. However, Dawkins suggests that human beings can assert their autonomy in the face of this genetic determinism. We are able to rebel against these selfish genes: 'We have the power to defy the selfish genes of our birth . . . We have the power to turn against our creators. We, alone on earth, can rebel against the tyranny of the selfish replicators.'[8] Human beings alone have evolved to the point at which we are able to rebel against and perhaps even take control of the process that brought us here in the first place.

Like many readers of *The Selfish Gene* I often find myself wondering whether Dawkins's optimistic conclusion isn't actually contradicted and subverted by the arguments that precede it. In some ways his analysis echoes the ethos of the Enlightenment: once you have understood something, you can master it. But can we master *ourselves* in this way? What if our genetic inheritance affects our will, so that we can recognize the hidden influence of our genes, while then discovering that we cannot break free from their influence?

Now Dawkins would resist any attempt on my part to suggest he has theological interests. Yet I – and others – have noticed a clear resonance between his narrative of genetic entrapment and the Christian one of captivity to sin.[9] In Dawkins's terms, the question is whether we can break free from the baleful influence of our evolutionary history; in theological terms, it is whether religious conversion delivers us from our past or whether this remains something that needs to be addressed continually throughout the life of faith. This lay at the heart of Augustine of Hippo's concerns about the views of Pelagius and his circle in the early fifth century. Augustine held that conversion did not allow people to break free totally from their past habits and passions, which remained a lingering presence in the life of faith. Pelagius believed that such past influences could be discarded and that they played no continuing role in redeemed existence.[10]

Yet Dawkins also engages with another aspect of human nature, namely the apparently natural tendency for human beings to be religious.[11] Once more he turns to a Darwinian metanarrative to explain this observation, arguing that the human cognitive processes that give rise to religion actually evolved for other purposes. Religion is an accidental and unnecessary by-product of these processes, arising from a 'misfiring' of something that originally served a useful purpose in ensuring our survival as a species.[12]

It's an interesting point, though lacking evidential warrant on the one hand and any empirically warranted definition of 'religion' on the other.[13] Any philosophy of life – such as Confucianism or Stoicism – is capable of being explained away on the same inadequate basis. And just as importantly, human civilization is characterized by a series of other enterprises that are culturally important but can also be asserted to be accidental by-products of evolution – including the scientific method itself.[14]

Lewis: longing for a true homeland

So what of Lewis? He is strongly critical of reductionist accounts of human nature, which shrink human significance to that of our basic chemical components. Sure, both human beings and amoebae are composed of atoms and molecules. Both are made up of the same elemental building blocks of the universe. Yet they are fundamentally different. Lewis highlights this point in his *Voyage of the Dawn Treader*. Eustace Scrubb proudly shows off his scientific knowledge of astronomy to Ramandu, an old man who lives on an island at the eastern edge of the world of Narnia. 'In our world,' said Eustace, 'a star is a huge ball of flaming gas.' The old man was not impressed: 'Even in your world, my son, that is not what a star is, but only what it is made of.'[15]

Lewis challenges the validity and utility of scientifically reductive accounts of human nature. He allows that these may help us understand aspects of human functionality – for example, how oxygen transport works – but argues that they are incapable of disclosing the full picture of who we are and why we are here. A purely materialist account of human nature ends up reducing our deepest beliefs and aspirations to the outcomes of chemical or electrical events in the human cortex, which is itself the by-product of a blind evolutionary process.

This question featured prominently in Lewis's conversations and correspondence with Sheldon Vanauken, a visiting student at Oxford University who was inclined to materialism. If Vanauken was the product of a materialistic universe, Lewis asked him, how come he didn't feel at home in that universe? Surely his deepest feelings and intuitions suggested there was more to life than this? 'We aren't adapted to it, not at home in it. If that is so, it may appear as a proof, or at least a powerful suggestion, that eternity exists and is our home.'[16]

For Lewis, any scientific account of human nature is inadequate. It needs to be supplemented by something deeper: knowledge of where we really *belong* and what we really *mean.*

Our deepest intuitions affirm that we are passing through this world – that we belong somewhere else. As a younger man, Lewis had been haunted by a deep intuition that his minimalist atheism failed to do justice to the complexities of the universe. He found himself reflecting on the possible implications of a profound and elusive sense of longing, heightened rather than satisfied by what he found around him and seemingly pointing to a world beyond the boundaries of human knowledge and experience: 'If I find in myself a desire which no experience in this world can satisfy, the most probable explanation is that I was made for another world.'[17]

For Lewis, the Christian faith entails the recognition of two quite different worlds or realms, namely the real world in which we live out our present lives, and another world we know through anticipation and expectation – hinted at by our experience of this world but lying tantalizingly beyond our reach. There is a wall between us and our true destiny – but there is a door in that wall:

> At present we are on the outside of the world, the wrong side of the door. We discern the freshness and purity of morning, but they do not make us fresh and pure. We cannot mingle with the splendours we see. But all the leaves of the New Testament are rustling with the rumour that it will not always be so. Some day, God willing, we shall get in.[18]

The contrast with Dawkins at this point is dramatic. For Dawkins, this universe defines the limits of reality. There is nothing beyond this world, and we need to face up to this bleak truth about our singular purposeless universe and get used to it. Lewis, however, picks up on an image – used by Plato – of a group of people who have lived all their lives in a dark underground cave, illuminated only by the flickering of a fire that casts shadows on the cave's walls.[19] They believe this dark and smoky realm defines the limits of reality, unaware of the brilliant world of sunlight and fresh air beyond its walls. And what if the world of the cave is vibrant with hints, signs and rumours of that other world, prompting us to explore things more deeply?

Reflecting on Dawkins and Lewis

A remark by the French philosopher Jacques Rancière helpfully focuses a core question about humanity over which Dawkins and Lewis disagree: 'The political question is first of all that of the ability of any body to seize hold of its destiny.'[20] Having worked out what life is all about, can we take hold of this vision of reality and achieve it? Or does the disclosure of this vision bring about a realization that it lies tantalizingly beyond our grasp?

Dawkins concluded *The Selfish Gene* with a dramatic declaration of the human need to break free from the 'tyranny of the selfish replicators'. How can we do this? For Dawkins, we must heal ourselves, and the motivation to do this must come from within – after all, as a good humanist he holds that there is no inspiration outside our own humanity.[21] That humanity can set its goals and achieve them without reference to or dependence on God is a common theme in secular humanist writings.

Yet can we really overcome our own flaws, biases, self-interest and weakness? Dawkins's Universal Darwinism highlights the importance of our evolutionary history, a hidden influence on our beliefs and actions that we can never entirely eliminate. Others might want to modify Dawkins at this point – with, for example, Keith E. Stanovich's argument that while we may be robots whose primary biological function is to serve as vehicles for genes, our higher-level analytic reasoning abilities are good enough to allow us to rebel against our genetically programmed systems as well as the cultural memes that infect and shape our rational minds.[22] Rational thought, Stanovich argues, can thus be used to override the sometimes self-destructive inclinations of our more primitive inherited intuitions.

Some Christians would see this as offering an important role for religion as a constituent element in this revolt against our genetic inheritance. Christian ideas and values do indeed offer a powerful alternative to a 'survival of the fittest' mentality – whether framed in intellectual terms or seen as embodied and exemplified in the life of Christ. The traditional notion of the 'mind of Christ' links together both ideas about Christ and an alignment of the believer's life with that of Christ.[23] Some early Christian writers – such as Clement of Alexandria and Irenaeus of Lyons – develop ideas that could bring about a mindset resistant to the kind of hidden genetic impulses and influences Dawkins describes.

Lewis, however, is cautious at this point, holding that we must acknowledge our entrapment and entanglement with sin. We are damaged and wounded and cannot heal ourselves. What is required is more than an adjustment of our thinking and recalibration of our intuitions (though Lewis concedes their importance). For Lewis, we are ill and need to be healed; we are damaged and need to be made whole.

In *Mere Christianity*, Lewis considers why salvation cannot be reduced simply to the impartation of corrective information or to adopting an ethic of self-improvement. What is required is rather more radical, namely a transformation of our situation, which is not merely something we cannot achieve by ourselves but something already done for us, if we reach out and embrace it:

We have not got to try to climb up into spiritual life by our own efforts; it has already come down into the human race. If we will only lay ourselves open to the one Man in whom it was fully present, and who, in spite of being God, is also a real man, He will do it in us and for us.[24]

Building on the idea that we need to be healed, Lewis develops the analogy of a 'good infection' – actually a reworking of Athanasius of Alexandria's classic argument in his *On the Incarnation*: 'Remember what I said about "good infection". One of our own race has this new life: if we get close to Him we shall catch it from Him.'[25] The question Lewis wants to answer is this: How can the life of Christ be 'spread' to other people?

His metaphor of good infection brings together the ideas of *proximity to* and *contact with* Christ, both integral to Athanasius's discussion of redemption. The metaphor avoids the inadequate idea that Christ is simply a teacher or moral influence; for Lewis, he is also the agent of transformation, which includes – but is not limited to – a change in the way we think. Literature is rich in terms of imaginative possibilities for visualizing this process – such as Cicero's notion of the 'infectious' power of example.[26] Although Lewis does not clarify this mechanism of transformation further, his language points to sin primarily in terms of entrapment and degradation, and salvation in terms of liberation and fulfilment.

So why are the issues raised by Dawkins and Lewis so important? This question concerns whether we as human beings are able to achieve the goals we believe are important – or whether we are rendered incapable of desiring and grasping them by some influence over us. Dawkins and Lewis disagree on the goals we should be pursuing; both, however, recognize problems in attaining them, reflecting limitations placed on human nature itself through the lingering influence of our evolutionary past (Dawkins) or through being held captive by sin (Lewis).

What are the answers? Some within the growing transhumanist movement suggest that the technological enhancement of humanity might lead to the suppression or even elimination of the influence of our genetic past, so that we can be 'rebooted' – and thus break free from genetic entrapment of the kind Dawkins notes. It's an approach that fits neatly into the philosopher Mary Midgley's category of 'science as salvation'.[27] Lewis offers a Christian alternative: we need to undergo healing, renewal and repair – and we cannot fix ourselves. Through faith we embrace a new way of thinking and living that is not of our own making but opens the way to becoming what we are meant to be.

Conclusion: searching for meaning

Sir Peter Medawar (1915–87), a leading British biologist who championed the public engagement of science, highlighted the importance of transcendence in the human quest for meaning. We long to see ourselves as part of a bigger picture that stretches beyond our immediate needs and concerns. Science is part of that picture – but only part: 'Only humans find their way by a light that illuminates more than the patch of ground they stand on.'[1] Medawar isn't on his own here. Salman Rushdie speaks of the longing of the human spirit to find significance 'outside the confines of its material, physical existence'.[2] Human beings seem to be driven to find something deeper than what can be found through an examination of the empirical world. That's what the human quest for meaning is all about.

Other voices could easily be brought into this conversation. One of the most interesting is that of Albert Einstein, who held that questions of personal meaning and ethical values are beyond the scope of the natural sciences:

> . . . the scientific method can teach us nothing beyond how facts are related to, and conditioned by, each other . . . knowledge of what *is* does not open the door directly to what *should be*. One can have the clearest and most complete knowledge of what *is*, and yet not be able to deduct from that what should be the *goal* of our human aspirations.[3]

Both the identity of that goal and the motivation to reach it 'must come from another source'. Einstein was not an orthodox religious believer but was acutely aware of the need to have a deeper vision of reality than that disclosed by the natural sciences. A similar thought was expressed by the Cambridge physicist Alexander Wood, who highlighted the capacity of a religious world view to disclose the intelligibility and coherence of our existence: 'This is our first demand of religion – that it should illumine life and make it a whole.'[4]

It's understandable that so many should focus on the question of what is distinctive about human nature, and try to express this scientifically. Yet this sometimes leads us to overlook questions about what human beings seem to need if they are to function properly. What does it mean to be human? Why is there evil and suffering? How do I find truth? What is a good life and how do I lead it? These can be treated as if they are *scientific* questions, but they're not. At heart they're *existential* questions. Although they may find philosophical answers, they are most naturally framed in terms of religion.[5]

Let's look at a personal history that highlights some of these points. Paul Kalanithi (1977–2015) was a promising neurosurgeon who died of metastatic lung cancer at the age of 37, before he could ever practise as a fully qualified surgeon. Once he knew he was dying, Kalanithi reflected long and hard on the meaning of life, the importance of the practice of medicine and the place of science in human culture. His bestselling book, *When Breath Becomes Air*, was written during his final illness and published posthumously.

Kalanithi loved science but found that it failed to engage with some of the questions that both really mattered to him and increased in importance as his illness progressed:

> Science may provide the most useful way to organize empirical, reproducible data, but its power to do so is predicated on its inability to grasp the most central aspects

of human life: hope, fear, love, hate, beauty, envy, honor, weakness, striving, suffering, virtue.[6]

Literature, however, illuminated experience, providing a way of confronting the 'messiness and weight of real human life'.[7] Kalanithi found writers such as T. S. Eliot helpful in exploring life's more complex questions, where other approaches were as 'dry as a bone'.[8]

Now Kalanithi may not be representative, although the huge impact of his book suggests that his personal story and the ideas that emerged from it resonate with many people. Science, he argues, is not really about explanation but about reducing phenomena into manageable units. By its very nature it cannot engage with the 'existential, visceral nature of human life, which is unique and subjective'.[9] There's nothing wrong with science; it's simply that its answers are important in some areas of life but not in others. To deal with the complexity of life we need more than science.

If we make science the arbiter of metaphysics, as Kalanithi notes, we 'banish not only God from the world but also love, hate, meaning', ending up with a world 'self-evidently *not* the world we live in'.[10] To deal with the many questions and challenges of real life – rather than those played with in philosophy seminars – we need more than one conceptual toolbox. That's one of the reasons why so many people try to find a way to hold science and faith together and create a more comprehensive and satisfying understanding of ourselves and our world.

So how does reading Kalanithi's poignant and deeply moving book help us reflect on Dawkins and Lewis? As a neurosurgeon, Kalanithi clearly affirms the importance of the natural sciences as a way of understanding how our world works, and as a means of developing new approaches to diagnosis and therapy. Yet he refuses to exalt science into a world view that establishes meaning and value. Those must come from other sources. He nods here in the directions of both Dawkins and Lewis, even if his more significant inspiration comes from the position represented by Lewis.

The great questions of life remain debated and discussed precisely because they are so important and because they transcend the evidential and rational capacities of human beings. It is easy to retreat into what, as we noted, Lewis styled a 'glib and shallow rationalism' – only to discover that its logical precision is achieved at the price of forfeiting any traction on the most meaningful questions of human existence. We ought to know how we and our universe work; yet we also need to know what they mean. For Lewis, the Christian narrative allows us to hold together the functionality and meaning of our universe.

This short book can only begin to open up these questions, allowing the very different ideas of Dawkins and Lewis to be compared and explored. How can we meet Dawkins's demand to show that our beliefs are justified, like those of the natural sciences? Or Lewis's concern that we do not limit ourselves to what the natural sciences can disclose? For Lewis, 'reason is the natural organ of truth; but imagination is the organ of meaning'[11] – and we need both if we are to find our way to something both true and trustworthy on the one hand yet capable of helping us find meaning on the other. Our journey of exploration and reflection continues!

Notes

Introduction

1 See especially Alister E. McGrath, *C. S. Lewis – A Life: Eccentric Genius, Reluctant Prophet* (London: Hodder & Stoughton, 2013) and *Dawkins' God: From the Selfish Gene to the God Delusion*, 2nd edn (Oxford: Wiley-Blackwell, 2015).

2 <www.salon.com/2015/02/08/the_perils_of_pressing_send_has_ richard_dawkins_ruined_his_legacy_partner>.

1 Big pictures: why meaning matters

1 Joshua A. Hicks and Laura A. King, 'Meaning in Life and Seeing the Big Picture', *Cognition and Emotion* 21:7 (2007), pp. 1577–84.

2 Jeanette Winterson, *Why Be Happy When You Could Be Normal?* (London: Vintage, 2012), p. 68.

3 Friedrich Nietzsche, *Götzen-Dämmerung; oder Wie man mit dem Hammer philosophiert* (Munich: Hanser, 1954), p. 7.

4 Keith Yandell, *Philosophy of Religion: A Contemporary Introduction* (London: Routledge, 1999), p. 16.

5 William D. Joske, 'Philosophy and the Meaning of Life', *Australasian Journal of Philosophy* 52:2 (1974), pp. 93–104.

6 Richard Dawkins, 'Universal Darwinism', in D. S. Bendall (ed.), *Evolution: From Molecules to Men* (Cambridge: Cambridge University Press, 1983), pp. 403–25.

7 Richard Dawkins, *The God Delusion* (London: Bantam, 2006), p. 188.

8 Richard Dawkins, *River out of Eden: A Darwinian View of Life* (London: Phoenix, 1995), p. 133.

9 Richard Dawkins, *An Appetite for Wonder* (London: Bantam, 2013), pp. 140–1.

10 Dawkins, *An Appetite for Wonder*, p. 141.

11 Dawkins, *An Appetite for Wonder*, pp. 140–1.

12 Richard Dawkins, 'Alternative Thought for the Day', BBC Radio 4, 14 August 2003.

13 Massimo Pigliucci, 'New Atheism and the Scientistic Turn in the Atheism Movement', *Midwest Studies in Philosophy* 37:1 (2013), pp. 142–53, esp. p. 144.

14 Sam Harris, *The Moral Landscape* (London: Bantam, 2010).

15 John Maynard Smith, 'Science and Myth', *Natural History* 93:11 (1984), pp. 10–24.

16 Peter B. Medawar, *The Limits of Science* (Oxford: Oxford University Press, 1985), p. 66.

17 C. S. Lewis, *Surprised by Joy* (London: HarperCollins, 2002), p. 197.

18 C. S. Lewis, *Mere Christianity* (London: HarperCollins, 2016), p. viii.

19 Lewis, *Mere Christianity*, p. xv.

20 C. S. Lewis, ed. Lesley Walmsley, *Essay Collection: Faith, Christianity and the Church* (London: Collins, 2000), p. 21.

21 For Lewis's use of the Bible in shaping his big picture, see David L. Jeffrey, *Houses of the Interpreter: Reading Scripture, Reading Culture* (Waco, TX: Baylor University Press, 2003), pp. 181–94. For the importance of this theme in general, see Craig S. Keener, *The Mind of the Spirit: Paul's Approach to Transformed Thinking* (Grand Rapids, MI: Baker, 2016).

22 Mark McIntosh, 'Faith, Reason and the Mind of Christ', in Paul J. Griffiths and Reinhart Hütter (eds), *Reason and the Reasons of Faith* (New York: T. & T. Clark, 2005), pp. 119–42.

23 Michael Ward, 'The Good Serves the Better and Both the Best: C. S. Lewis on Imagination and Reason in Apologetics', in Andrew Davison (ed.), *Imaginative Apologetics: Theology, Philosophy and the Catholic Tradition* (London: SCM Press, 2011), pp. 59–78; Alister E. McGrath, *The Intellectual World of C. S. Lewis* (Oxford: Wiley-Blackwell, 2013), 'Reason, Experience, and Imagination: Lewis's Apologetic Method', pp. 129–46.

24 Lewis, *Mere Christianity*, p. 134.

25 See especially Ann Taves, Egil Asprem and Elliott Ihm, 'Psychology, Meaning Making, and the Study of World Views: Beyond Religion and Non-Religion', *Psychology of Religion and Spirituality* 10:3 (2018), pp. 207–17.

26 See, for example, Alister McGrath, *Mere Discipleship: On Growing in Wisdom and Hope* (London: SPCK, 2018).

27 Iris Murdoch, *Metaphysics as A Guide To Morals* (London: Chatto & Windus, 1992), p. 7.

28 Salman Rushdie, *Is Nothing Sacred? The Herbert Read Memorial Lecture 1990* (Cambridge: Granta, 1990), p. 9.

29 Ludwig Wittgenstein, *Philosophical Investigations*, 4th edn (Oxford: Wiley-Blackwell, 2009), §115; emphasis in original.

30 David Egan, 'Pictures in Wittgenstein's Later Philosophy', *Philosophical Investigations* 34:1 (2011), pp. 55–76.

31 See especially Peter Harrison, *The Territories of Science and Religion* (Chicago: University of Chicago Press, 2015), pp. 172–6, 191–8.

32 Dawkins, *The God Delusion*, pp. 66–9.

33 J. R. R. Tolkien, *Tree and Leaf* (London: HarperCollins, 2001), pp. 71–2.

34 For a detailed analysis, see Alister E. McGrath, *The Intellectual World of C. S. Lewis* (Oxford: Wiley-Blackwell, 2013), 'A Gleam of Divine Truth: The Concept of Myth in Lewis's Thought', pp. 55–82.

35 For a justification and exploration of this view, see Alister E. McGrath, *Enriching Our Vision of Reality: Theology and the Natural Sciences in Dialogue* (London: SPCK, 2016).

36 For a good account, see Michael Ward, 'Science and Religion in the Writings of C. S. Lewis', *Science and Christian Belief* 25:1 (2013), pp. 3–16.

2 Reasoned belief: faith, proof and evidence

1 Thomas Nagel, *The Last Word* (Oxford: Oxford University Press, 1997), p. 130.

2 Bertrand Russell, *Mortals and Others: Bertrand Russell's American Essays, 1931–1935*, vol. 2 (London: Routledge, 1998), p. 28.

3 Bertrand Russell, *A History of Western Philosophy* (London: Allen & Unwin, 1946), p. xiv.

4 For the details, see Alister McGrath, *The Intellectual World of C. S. Lewis* (Oxford: Wiley-Blackwell, 2013), 'Reason, Experience, and Imagination: Lewis's Apologetic Method', pp. 129–46.

5 The four short quotations in this paragraph are from C. S. Lewis, *Mere Christianity* (London: HarperCollins, 2016), pp. 25 (two), 21 and 137 respectively.

6 C. S. Lewis, *Surprised by Joy* (London: HarperCollins, 2002), p. 249.

7 Ludwig Wittgenstein, *On Certainty* (Oxford: Blackwell, 1974), p. 98.

8 C. S. Lewis, *The Problem of Pain* (London: Centenary Press, 1940) and *A Grief Observed* (London: Faber & Faber, 1961).

9 Lewis, *Mere Christianity*, pp. 136–7. See further Alister E. McGrath, 'The Rationality of Faith: How Does Christianity Make Sense of Things?', *Philosophia Christi* 18:2 (2016), pp. 395–408.

10 Richard Dawkins, *A Devil's Chaplain* (London: Weidenfeld & Nicholson, 2003), p. 117.

11 Richard Dawkins, *The Selfish Gene*, 2nd edn (Oxford: Oxford University Press, 1989), p. 198.

12 One of the best studies of Dawkins on this point is Michael Shermer, 'The Skeptic's Chaplain: Richard Dawkins as a Fountainhead of Skepticism', in Alan Grafen and Mark Ridley (eds), *Richard Dawkins: How a Scientist Changed the Way We Think* (Oxford: Oxford University Press, 2006), pp. 227–35.

13 Reproduced in Dawkins, *A Devil's Chaplain*, p. 248.

14 It is interesting to explore Dawkins's somewhat naive scientific positivism in the light of the critical philosophical analysis set out in Thomas Bonk, *Underdetermination: An Essay on Evidence and the Limits of Natural Knowledge* (Dordrecht: Springer, 2008).

15 Dawkins, *The Selfish Gene*, p. 330.

16 For a collection of essays from leading thinkers exploring the options, see Bernard Carr (ed.), *Universe or Multiverse?* (Cambridge: Cambridge University Press, 2007).

17 Maximilian Schlosshauer, Johannes Kofler and Anton Zeilinger, 'A Snapshot of Foundational Attitudes toward Quantum Mechanics', *Studies in the History and Philosophy of Modern Physics* 44:3 (2013), pp. 220–30.

18 For a good history of this development, see Helge Kragh, *Conceptions of Cosmos: From Myths to the Accelerating Universe* (Oxford: Oxford University Press, 2007).

19 Debate between Richard Dawkins and Steven Pinker at Westminster Central Hall, London, 19 February 1999, chaired by Tim Radford, science correspondent of *The Guardian*.

20 For a more recent critique of this scientific 'fantasy', see Roger Penrose, *Fashion, Faith, and Fantasy in the New Physics of the Universe* (Princeton, NJ: Princeton University Press, 2017).

21 For the importance of Narnia in this respect, see the excellent study of Rowan Williams, *The Lion's World: A Journey into the Heart of Narnia* (London: SPCK, 2012).

22 See note 8 above.

23 See Ann Loades, 'The Grief of C. S. Lewis', *Theology Today* 46:3 (1989), pp. 269–76.

24 Timothy P. Burt, 'Homogenising the Rainfall Record at Durham for the 1870s', *Hydrological Sciences Journal* 54:1 (2009), pp. 199–209.

25 J. R. de Laeter et al., 'Atomic Weights of the Elements: Review 2000 (IUPAC Technical Report)', *Pure and Applied Chemistry* 75:6 (2003), pp. 683–800.

26 For the complexity of this true statement, see Barbara Abbott, 'Water = H_2O', *Mind* 108:429 (1999), pp. 145–8.

27 Bertrand Russell, *Bertrand Russell Speaks his Mind* (London: Barker, 1960), p. 20 and *Essays in Skepticism* (New York: Philosophical Library, 1963), pp. 83–4.

28 Dawkins, *The God Delusion* (London: Bantam, 2006), pp. 50–1. Dawkins indicates a degree of sympathy for this position but indicates he would also consider himself a 'strong atheist' – that is, someone who can say 'I know there is no God.'

29 John Polkinghorne, *Theology in the Context of Science* (New Haven, CT: Yale University Press, 2009), pp. 125–6.

30 Polkinghorne, *Theology in the Context of Science*, p. 126.

31 For a recording of this debate, see <https://podcasts.ox.ac.uk/nature-human-beings-and-question-their-ultimate-origin>.

32 Alain de Botton, *Religion for Atheists: A Non-Believer's Guide to the Uses of Religion* (London: Penguin, 2013).

33 Dawkins, *The Selfish Gene*, p. 198.

34 Dawkins, *The God Delusion*, p. 308.

35 Lewis, *Surprised by Joy*, p. 197.

36 See the insightful essay of Gilbert Meilaender, 'Theology in Stories: C. S. Lewis and the Narrative Quality of Experience', *Word and World* 1:3 (1981), pp. 222–30.

3 Is there a God?

1 Aristotle, *Rhetoric* 1356 b 28.

2 Daniel C. Dennett, *Breaking the Spell: Religion as a Natural Phenomenon* (New York: Viking Penguin, 2006), p. 9.

3 Donovan Schaefer, 'Blessed, Precious Mistakes: Deconstruction, Evolution, and New Atheism in America', *International Journal for Philosophy of Religion* 76:1 (2014), pp. 75–94.

4 For the scholarship, see Jonathan Jong, 'On (Not) Defining (Non) Religion', *Science, Religion and Culture* 2:3 (2015), pp. 15–24.

5 Richard Dawkins, *The God Delusion* (London: Bantam, 2006); these points are explored in detail in the chapter on why 'there almost certainly is no God', pp. 111–59.

6   Lawrence Sklar, *Space, Time, and Spacetime* (Berkeley, CA: University of California Press, 1977), p. 162.

7   Richard Swinburne, *Simplicity as Evidence for Truth* (Milwaukee, WI: Marquette University Press, 1997).

8   See Hauke Riesch, 'Simple or Simplistic? Scientists' Views on Occam's Razor', *Theoria* 25:1 (2010), pp. 75–90.

9   William Ralph Inge, *Faith and Its Psychology* (New York: Charles Scribner's Sons, 1910), p. 197.

10 Dawkins, *The God Delusion*, p. 108. This god is elsewhere described as a 'psychotic delinquent' (p. 38) and a 'cruel ogre' (p. 250).

11 A point made forcefully by Katharine Dell, *Who Needs the Old Testament? Its Enduring Appeal and Why the New Atheists Don't Get It* (London: SPCK, 2017).

12 C. S. Lewis, *Mere Christianity* (London: HarperCollins, 2016), p. 38.

13 C. S. Lewis, ed. Lesley Walmsley, *Essay Collection: Faith, Christianity and the Church* (London: Collins, 2000), pp. 213–14.

14 Lewis, *Mere Christianity*, p. 175.

15 Lewis, *Mere Christianity*, p. 176.

16 I explore this theme in Alister McGrath, *Mere Discipleship: Growing in Wisdom and Hope* (London: SPCK, 2018).

17 C. S. Lewis, ed. Walter Hooper, *Selected Literary Essays* (Cambridge: Cambridge University Press, 1969; repr. 2013), 'Bluspels and Flalansferes: A Semantic Nightmare', p. 265.

18 C. S. Lewis, *Studies in Medieval and Renaissance Literature* (Cambridge: Cambridge University Press, 1966), 'Imagery in the Last Eleven Cantos of Dante's *Comedy*', pp. 78–93; quote at p. 90.

19 Ludwig Wittgenstein, *On Certainty* (Oxford: Blackwell, 1974), p. 98.

20 Richard Dawkins, *River out of Eden: A Darwinian View of Life* (London: Phoenix, 1995), p. 133.

21 Bertrand Russell, *A History of Western Philosophy* (London: Allen & Unwin, 1946), p. xiv.

22 Drusilla Scott, *Everyman Revived: The Common Sense of Michael Polanyi* (Grand Rapids, MI: Eerdmans, 1995), p. 60.

23 See the excellent study of Basil Willey on Tennyson's exploration of the interface of faith and doubt in Basil Willey, *More Nineteenth Century Studies* (London: Chatto & Windus, 1956), pp. 79–105.

24 Tennyson, 'The Ancient Sage', lines 66–7. For the best discussion of this rich and insightful poem, see Howard W. Fulweiler, 'The Argument of "The Ancient Sage": Tennyson and the Christian Intellectual Tradition', *Victorian Poetry* 21:3 (1983), pp. 203–16.

25 John Gray, *Seven Types of Atheism* (London: Penguin Books, 2018), p. 158.

26 Fraser N. Watts, *Psychology, Religion, and Spirituality: Concepts and Applications* (Cambridge: Cambridge University Press, 2017), p. 83.

27 For the details, see Alister McGrath, *C. S. Lewis – A Life: Eccentric Genius, Reluctant Prophet* (London: Hodder & Stoughton, 2013), pp. 67–73.

28 Dawkins, *The God Delusion*, p. 31.

29 Christopher Hitchens, *God Is Not Great: How Religion Poisons Everything* (New York: Twelve, 2007), p. 8.

30 Hitchens, *God Is Not Great*, p. 10.

31 Josef Winiger, *Ludwig Feuerbach: Denker der Menschlichkeit: Eine Biographie* (Berlin: Aufbau Taschenbuch Verlag, 2004).

32 Bernard Williams, *Morality: An Introduction to Ethics* (Cambridge: Cambridge University Press, 1993), p. 80; emphasis in original.

33 Algernon Charles Swinburne, 'Hymn of Man', in *Songs before Sunrise* (London: F. S. Ellis, 1871), p. 124.

34 Bertrand Russell, *Unpopular Essays* (New York: Routledge, 1996), p. 82.

4 Human nature: who are we?

1 Amartya Sen, *Identity and Violence: The Illusion of Destiny* (New York: Norton, 2006), p. 19.

2 Jenny McGill, *Religious Identity and Cultural Negotiation: Toward a Theology of Christian Identity in Migration* (Eugene, OR: Pickwick Publications, 2016).

3 See Paul Erickson, Judy L. Klein, Lorraine Daston, Rebecca M. Lemov, Thomas Sturm and Michael D. Gordin, *How Reason Almost Lost Its Mind: The Strange Career of Cold War Rationality* (Chicago: University of Chicago Press, 2013).

4 Typewritten text of 1966 reproduced in Richard Dawkins, *An Appetite for Wonder: The Making of a Scientist: A Memoir* (London: Bantam, 2013), p. 200; emphasis in original.

5 Dawkins, *The Selfish Gene*, 2nd edn (Oxford: Oxford University Press, 1989), pp. 9–10.

6 Richard Dawkins, *River out of Eden: A Darwinian View of Life* (London: Phoenix, 1995), p. 133.

7 Dawkins, *The Selfish Gene*, p. 10; emphasis in original.

8 Dawkins, *The Selfish Gene*, pp. 200–1.

9   See, for example, Marie Vejrup Nielsen, *Sin and Selfish Genes: Christian and Biological Narratives* (Leuven: Peeters, 2010).

10 See Nicholas Rengger, *The Anti-Pelagian Imagination in Political Theory and International Relations: Dealing in Darkness* (London: Routledge, 2017), pp. 1–9.

11 For an excellent discussion of this tendency, see Pascal Boyer, *The Naturalness of Religious Ideas: A Cognitive Theory of Religion* (Berkeley, CA: University of California Press, 1994).

12 Richard Dawkins, *The God Delusion* (London: Bantam, 2006), p. 188.

13 Peter J. Richerson and Lesley Newson, 'Is Religion Adaptive? Yes, No, Neutral. But Mostly We Don't Know', in Jeffrey Schloss and Michael Murray (eds), *The Believing Primate: Scientific, Philosophical and Theological Reflections on the Origin of Religion* (Oxford: Oxford University Press, 2009), pp. 100–17.

14 Justin L. Barrett, 'Is the Spell Really Broken? Bio-Psychological Explanations of Religion and Theistic Belief', *Theology and Science* 5:1 (2007), pp. 57–72.

15 C. S. Lewis, *The Voyage of the Dawn Treader* (London: HarperCollins, 2009), p. 215.

16 C. S. Lewis (ed. Walter Hooper), *Collected Letters* (London: HarperCollins, 2004–6), vol. 3, p. 76.

17 C. S. Lewis, *Mere Christianity* (London: HarperCollins, 2016), pp. 136–7.

18 C. S. Lewis, ed. Lesley Walmsley, *Essay Collection: Faith, Christianity and the Church* (London: Collins, 2000), p. 104.

19 For Lewis's use of Plato, see William G. Johnson and Marcia K. Houtman, 'Platonic Shadows in C. S. Lewis' Narnia Chronicles', *Modern Fiction Studies* 32:1 (1986), pp. 75–87, esp. pp. 78–81.

20 Jacques Rancière, *Le spectateur émancipé* (Paris: La Fabrique, 2008), p. 88.

21 See Richard Norman, *On Humanism* (London: Routledge, 2012), pp. 162–3.

22 Keith E. Stanovich, *The Robot's Rebellion: Finding Meaning in the Age of Darwin* (Chicago: University of Chicago Press, 2004).

23 Mark McIntosh, 'Faith, Reason and the Mind of Christ', in Paul J. Griffiths and Reinhart Hütter (eds), *Reason and the Reasons of Faith* (New York: T. & T. Clark, 2005).

24 Lewis, *Mere Christianity*, pp. 181–2.

25 Lewis, *Mere Christianity*, p. 182. There are also, of course, important parallels with Augustine of Hippo's thinking on sin and redemption:

see Jesse Couenhoven, *Stricken by Sin, Cured by Christ: Agency, Necessity, and Culpability in Augustinian Theology* (New York: Oxford University Press, 2013).

26 For the literary background to such metaphors, see Peta Mitchell, *Contagious Metaphor* (London: Continuum, 2012).

27 Mary Midgley, *Science as Salvation: A Modern Myth and Its Meaning* (London: Routledge, 1992).

Conclusion: searching for meaning

1 Peter B. Medawar and Jean Medawar, *The Life Science: Current Ideas of Biology* (London: Wildwood House, 1977), p. 171.

2 Salman Rushdie, *Is Nothing Sacred? The Herbert Read Memorial Lecture 1990* (Cambridge: Granta, 1990), p. 7.

3 Albert Einstein, *Ideas and Opinions* (New York: Crown Publishers, 1954), 'Science and Religion', pp. 41–2. For further discussion, see Max Jammer, *Einstein and Religion: Physics and Theology* (Princeton, NJ: Princeton University Press, 1999); emphasis in original.

4 Alexander Wood, *In Pursuit of Truth: A Comparative Study in Science and Religion* (London: Student Christian Movement, 1927), p. 102.

5 See Dariusz Krok, 'The Role of Meaning in Life Within the Relations of Religious Coping and Psychological Well-Being', *Journal of Religion and Health* 54:6 (2015), pp. 2292–308.

6 Paul Kalanithi, *When Breath Becomes Air* (London: Vintage Books, 2017), p. 170.

7 Kalanithi, *When Breath Becomes Air*, pp. 30–1.

8 Kalanithi, *When Breath Becomes Air*, p. 31.

9 Kalanithi, *When Breath Becomes Air*, p. 170.

10 Kalanithi, *When Breath Becomes Air*, p. 169; emphasis in original.

11 C. S. Lewis, ed. Walter Hooper, *Selected Literary Essays* (Cambridge: Cambridge University Press, 1969; repr. 2013), 'Bluspels and Flalansferes: A Semantic Nightmare', p. 265.

For further reading

Works by or about Richard Dawkins

The three books most relevant to the questions raised in this volume are:

Dawkins, Richard, *The Blind Watchmaker: Why the Evidence of Evolution Reveals a Universe without Design* (New York: W. W. Norton, 1986).
———— *The God Delusion* (London: Bantam, 2006).
———— *The Selfish Gene*, 2nd edn (Oxford: Oxford University Press, 1989).

Two other works raise questions related to religious issues:

Dawkins, Richard, *A Devil's Chaplain: Selected Writings* (London: Weidenfeld & Nicholson, 2003).
———— *Unweaving the Rainbow: Science, Delusion and the Appetite for Wonder* (London: Penguin, 1998).

Works about Richard Dawkins relevant to this volume:

Elsdon-Baker, Fern, *The Selfish Genius: How Richard Dawkins Rewrote Darwin's Legacy* (London: Icon, 2009).
Grafen, Alan and Mark Ridley (eds), *Richard Dawkins: How a Scientist Changed the Way We Think* (Oxford: Oxford University Press, 2006).

For Dawkins's views on science and faith, see especially:

McGrath, Alister E., *Dawkins' God: From the Selfish Gene to the God Delusion*, 2nd edn (Oxford: Wiley-Blackwell, 2015).

Works by or about C. S. Lewis

The following are especially relevant to the topics discussed in this volume:

Lewis, C. S., *Mere Christianity* (London: HarperCollins, 2001).
——— *Surprised by Joy* (London: HarperCollins, 2001).

The following essays, included in C. S. Lewis, *Essay Collection: Faith, Christianity and the Church*, ed. Lesley Walmsley (London: HarperCollins, 2000), should also be noted:

'Is theology poetry?' (pp. 10–21)
'The Weight of Glory' (pp. 96–106)
'On Obstinacy in Belief' (pp. 206–15)

Works about C. S. Lewis relevant to this volume:

McGrath, Alister E., *C. S. Lewis – A Life: Eccentric Genius, Reluctant Prophet* (London: Hodder & Stoughton, 2013).
——— *The Intellectual World of C. S. Lewis* (Oxford: Wiley-Blackwell, 2013).
Williams, Rowan D., *The Lion's World: A Journey into the Heart of Narnia* (London: SPCK, 2012).

Other works that engage the questions opened up in this book

Aeschliman, Michael D., *The Restitution of Man: C. S. Lewis and the Case against Scientism* (Grand Rapids, MI: Eerdmans, 1998).
Gasper, Karen and Gerald L. Clore, 'Attending to the Big Picture: Mood and Global Versus Local Processing of Visual Information', *Psychological Science* 13:1 (2002), pp. 34–40.
Hicks, Joshua A. and Laura A. King, 'Meaning in Life and Seeing the Big Picture: Positive Affect and Global Focus', *Cognition and Emotion* 21:7 (2007), pp. 1577–84.
Kidd, Ian James, 'Receptivity to Mystery: Cultivation, Loss, and Scientism', *European Journal for Philosophy of Religion* 4:3 (2012), pp. 51–68.
McGrath, Alister E., 'An Enhanced Vision of Rationality: C. S. Lewis on the Reasonableness of Christian Faith', *Theology* 116:6 (2013), pp. 410–17.
Meilaender, Gilbert, 'Theology in Stories: C. S. Lewis and the Narrative Quality of Experience', *Word and World* 1:3 (1981), pp. 222–30.
Pigliucci, Massimo, 'New Atheism and the Scientistic Turn in the Atheism Movement', *Midwest Studies in Philosophy* 37:1 (2013), pp. 142–53.
Sacks, Jonathan, *The Great Partnership: God, Science and the Search for Meaning* (London: Hodder & Stoughton, 2011).

Tanzella-Nitti, Giuseppe, 'Religion and Science as Inclinations Toward the Search for Global Meaning', *Theology and Science* 10:2 (2012), pp. 167–78.

Trigg, Roger, *Beyond Matter: Why Science Needs Metaphysics* (West Conshohocken, PA: Templeton Press, 2015).

Ward, Michael, 'Science and Religion in the Writings of C. S. Lewis', *Science and Christian Belief* 25:1 (2013), pp. 3–16.

Wielenberg, Erik J., *God and the Reach of Reason: C. S. Lewis, David Hume, and Bertrand Russell* (Cambridge: Cambridge University Press, 2008).

Wolf, Susan R., *Meaning in Life* (Princeton, NJ: Princeton University Press, 2010).